WARSHIPS OF THE
BAY OF QUINTE

WARSHIPS OF THE
BAY OF QUINTE

ROGER LITWILLER

Mark,
Wonderful to meet & thank you for the tour.
Best of luck in your upcoming retirement.
Calm seas!

Cheers

DUNDURN
TORONTO

Editor: Matt Baker
Design: Jesse Hooper
Printer: Webcom

Library and Archives Canada Cataloguing in Publication

Litwiller, Roger
        Warships of the Bay of Quinte / Roger Litwiller.

Includes bibliographical references.
Issued also in electronic format.
ISBN 978-1-55488-929-7

        1. Warships--Canada--History--20th century. 2. World War, 1939-1945--Naval operations, Canadian. 3. Canada. Royal Canadian Navy--History--20th century--Sources. 4. Quinte, Bay of (Ont.)--History--20th century. I. Title.

VA400.L58 2011   359.0097109'043   C2011-900941-2

1   2   3   4   5   15   14   13   12   11

We acknowledge the support of the **Canada Council for the Arts** and the **Ontario Arts Council** for our publishing program. We also acknowledge the financial support of the **Government of Canada** through the **Canada Book Fund** and **Livres Canada Books**, and the **Government of Ontario** through the **Ontario Book Publishers Tax Credit** program, and the **Ontario Media Development Corporation**.

Care has been taken to trace the ownership of copyright material used in this book. The author and the publisher welcome any information enabling them to rectify any references or credits in subsequent editions.

J. Kirk Howard, President

Printed and bound in Canada.
www.dundurn.com

Dundurn Press
3 Church Street, Suite 500
Toronto, Ontario, Canada
M5E 1M2

Gazelle Book Services Limited
White Cross Mills
High Town, Lancaster, England
LA1 4XS

Dundurn Press
2250 Military Road
Tonawanda, NY
U.S.A. 14150

CONTENTS

FOREWORD

With this book, Roger Litwiller has very capably fleshed out the careers of six Canadian warships named for the Quinte-area municipalities. In so doing he has joined a dwindling coterie who have served our Navy with pride and afterward striven to keep its memory green. Welcome aboard and BRAVO ZULU, Roger!

Ken Macpherson
Port Hope
September 2010

ACKNOWLEDGEMENTS

*W*ARSHIPS OF THE BAY OF QUINTE is the first book that I have written, and the process has been a truly educational experience for me. On this quest, I was very fortunate to draw on the experience and tutoring of many respected individuals.

When I first became a sea cadet with RCSCC Warspite in 1977, Ken Macpherson's *Canada's Fighting Ships* was the only book on the Canadian Navy in the Kitchener Public Library. I was very fortunate to meet Ken a few years ago, and he graciously signed my copy of his book. I was similarly honoured when he agreed to write the foreword for *Warships* and edit the manuscript. Tony German, author of *The Sea Is at Our Gates*, has provided me with encouragement, direction, and has reviewed my work. Tony has opened many doors for me.

Dr. Paul Adamthwaite and his wife Betty-Ann, of the Archives and Collections Society in Picton, Ontario, have provided many hours of tutoring, as well as resources, experience, and introductions to several authors. Their encouragement and patience have allowed me to bring my project forward to completion.

It would be improper if I did not acknowledge the many archives and collections that I was able to draw resources and information from. I thank Library and Archives Canada as well as the Department of National Defence, Directorate of History and Heritage, for providing me with the resources to re-create the histories of the ships.

The stories of these ships came from many local archives and archivists: Robert Amasse, of the Quinte West Public Library in Trenton; Jane Foster, of the Lennox and Addington Museum in Napanee; Jeff Sumner, from the Thunder Bay Historical Museum Society; Richard Sanderson, with the Maritime Command Museum in Halifax; Ben Holthof, of the Marine Museum of the Great Lakes in Kingston; Mike Shortridge, from the Naval Museum of Manitoba; and finally, the Belleville Public Library.

Several individuals provided invaluable resources from their private collections, in the form of photographs, letters, and memories. Their contribution has taken this work from a history to a *story*. It would not be complete without the contributions of Richard Gimblett, Henry Winsor, Robert Hall, Bruce Keir, Jack Harold, Tom Farrell, Ida Campbell, Walter Gregory, Sam Andrews, Max Corkum, Gordon Gibbins, Roger Glassco, Sid Coates, Frank Barron, and Chuck Stevens.

Finally, I must thank my wife Rhonda and our children — Michelle, Shawn, Aaron, Cyndi, Brandon, and Alex — for their patience and understanding while I would disappear to Ottawa for a "few" days, or interrupt a family vacation for an interview or to crawl through an archives somewhere, sometimes to gain a single newspaper clipping. Their support and co-operation has given me the strength to complete this work.

INTRODUCTION

ARLY IN THE HISTORY OF THE CANADIAN Navy, we named our ships as did many of the world's navies: after famous people, places, or battles. Or as the Royal Navy have, with words of inspiration to strike fear into the enemy. Many of us know of such great ships as *Victory*, *Undaunted*, and *Fearless*.

During the Second World War, Canada changed this policy and began naming ships after communities in our country. The navy had to grow very large, very fast. The Canadian Navy started the war with six destroyers and 2,000 sailors, and before the war was over we had built the third largest navy in the world, with over 400 ships of all classes and over 100,000 men and women. We were able to build the ships and provide everything the men would need to go into battle with them, but not the comforts that make a ship a home, such as washing machines, magazines, books, mittens, writing materials, and so on. By attaching a ship to a community in name, it was hoped that the citizens of the community would have a direct bond to the ship and provide the men with all the comforts of home.

The change in naming policy had its intended effect, and soon it became a status symbol to have a ship named for your community, to the point that city councils would aggressively pursue the navy for this honour. Several communities would even petition the navy to completely man "their ship" with their own men. The navy refused with good reason: if the ship was ever lost, as several were, the loss of life for any one community would be devastating. Therefore, each ship in the Royal Canadian Navy was instead a cross-section of Canada. People of every province, major city, and small community could find someone they knew serving in many of the over 400 ships Canada ended the war with. This

fact is well-demonstrated in the history of HMCS *Trentonian* and the list of her crew on the nominal roll.

This book may appear to be a history of only the Bay of Quinte, but in reality the history of its six ships was written in the blood and sweat of Canadians from all across this great country.

I have included many personal stories by the men who served in these ships, but my focus is still the ships themselves; the personal stories are kept to a minimum, primarily to conserve space and prevent this book from becoming a "volume." All sailors know that a ship is a living, breathing entity, and it is the men who serve in her that give the ship her character, heart, and soul.

Together, the Bay of Quinte warships span almost 25 years of history in the Royal Canadian Navy and have participated is some of the major events that shaped its past, present, and future. One ship is credited with sinking two German submarines, another suffered serious damage off Cape Breton, and several met the enemy during various battles on the Atlantic Ocean, the English Channel, and at Normandy. Two of the ships went on to have a long career with other navies. The last ship to serve participated in the most deadly moment of the Cold War: the Cuban Missile Crisis. All but one returned to Canada at the end of their service.

Some of the ship names are still in use today. While no longer used to signify an active warship, they survive with a number of local Sea Cadet and Navy League Cadets Corps — with RCSCC Quinte in Belleville, RCSCC Napanee in Napanee, and NLCC Trentonian in Trenton.

I have attempted to use proper naval grammar and etiquette throughout this book. A ship is commonly referred to as "she" and is a proper name and

a noun; the word "the" is never used in relation to a
ship's name. You would never refer to a friend as "the
Michelle." Quotation marks are never used to identify
a ship's name. As a final note, whenever I first use a
naval term or reference I have attempted to explain
its meaning.

This book is dedicated to the ships and the men
who served in them. Together, they represented the
communities for which they were named, Canada,
and the Royal Canadian Navy with distinction and
pride. This ensures that names such as *Trentonian*,
Belleville, *Napanee*, *Hallowell*, and *Quinte* will always
be a part of Canada's proud naval heritage.

CHAPTER 1

A HISTORY

THE BAY OF QUINTE IS LOCATED ON the eastern end of Lake Ontario, between Toronto and Kingston, and almost entirely separates Prince Edward County from the rest of Ontario, forming the largest bay off Lake Ontario.

Several communities lie directly on the Bay, including Trenton, Belleville, Deseronto, Napanee, and Picton. Each of these communities has had strong ties to marine trade. In their early histories they relied on sailing ships and steamers to transport goods, materials, and citizens on the Bay to the rest of the world. This has all contributed to the Bay of Quinte's long civil marine history.

The area's naval history is just as long and rich. During the War of 1812 with the United States, warships used the Bay and surrounding waterways for passage up and down the lake. American warships would lie in wait near the False Duck Islands off the southeastern shore of Prince Edward County for ships of the Royal Navy to leave the protection of Kingston Harbour.

The most celebrated action during the War of 1812 involving the Bay of Quinte was the pursuit of HMS *Royal George*, at the time the largest warship on Lake Ontario. She was caught on the lake alone by the American squadron, and took refuge in the Bay of Quinte and surrounding islands overnight. The next day she made a dash for Kingston, with the U.S. warships following her close astern, exchanging cannon fire with the Americans all the way until she made the protection of the shore batteries. The Americans, not content to give up a prize, followed *Royal George* into the harbour and only retreated when the cannon fire from the area batteries and other ships started to find its mark on the U.S. ships.

Because of the war with the U.S. and continued fear of hostilities, a protected waterway was proposed: the Murray Canal. This was designed to move ships along the eastern end of Lake Ontario without exposing them to American naval forces and was completed at Carrying Place after the turn of the century. It is a seven-mile passage from the western end of the Bay of Quinte to Lake Ontario at Presqu'ile Bay, and has shortened the travel time ever since its construction by circumventing the long trip around Prince Edward County and the dangerous shoreline that faces the lake.

Also constructed at Trenton at the mouth of the Trent River was the Trent-Severn Waterway, a series of locks that stretched from Trenton to Port Severn, on Georgian Bay. This inland passage was originally designed to give commercial traffic a protected route to the upper Lakes, in case of renewed conflict with the Americans. The advantage to the waterway is avoiding most of Lake Ontario, Lake Erie, and Lake Huron, and it has shortened travel time to the upper Great Lakes considerably. With the arrival of the railroad, though, today both of these waterways are used almost exclusively for civilian traffic and pleasure boats.

Similarly, while marine construction was once well-established on the Bay of Quinte, changes in demand have scaled back operations. The last remaining shipbuilder, McNally Marine Incorporated, is located at Point Anne, just east of Belleville. This firm constructed the last *Maid of the Mist* for Niagara Falls. Today they build and repair barges and underwater pipelines.

The military has had a long-standing presence in the Quinte area, from the early French and English War, to the British regiments guarding the portage at Carrying Place at the western end of the Bay of Quinte. Fort Kente was established at Carrying Place with a garrison and field hospital during the War of 1812.

During the First World War, the largest ammunition and explosives factory in Canada was established in Trenton by the British Chemical Company. Located on a 255-acre site on the east side of the river near Number 1 Dam, the factory employed over 3,000 people from the area and manufactured TNT, gun cotton, sulphuric acid, nitric acid, and nitro-cellulose powder. Two hundred tons of TNT from Trenton was aboard the merchant ship SS *Mont Blanc* when she collided with a Norwegian ship in Halifax Harbour and exploded, destroying the city on 5 December 1917, and killing an estimated 2,000 people.

On Thanksgiving Day, 14 October 1918, a similar fate awaited Trenton. At 6:12 in the evening, the factory caught fire and the resulting explosions devastated the city. The fire could be seen as far away as Belleville, Picton, and Cobourg, with the explosions actually felt in Belleville, 20 kilometres away. Fortunately there were no lives lost and injuries were minimal, as the city and surrounding area were evacuated and the choice of Trenton for the plant was due to the location of a natural bunker formed by the surrounding hills, which forced the explosions up and over the surrounding area. The factory was never rebuilt, but in the same area a fireworks warehouse now stands.

During the Second World War, several factories were converted to support the navy: Central Bridge in Trenton built tugboats and barges along the Trent River, General Electric built motors, while north of Belleville, Corby's Distillery produced alcohol for the explosives used in depth charges and torpedoes.

Prior to this conversion, in the 1930s the area was witness to the construction of a large military base for the Royal Canadian Air Force. This resulted in the construction of several smaller airfields during the Second World War around the area and an influx of air crews from around the Commonwealth for flight training under the British Commonwealth Air Training Plan.

Trenton and the Bay of Quinte area continue a strong association with the Canadian Armed Forces and are known for Canada's Air Force and 8 Wing, CFB Trenton, overshadowing the long naval tradition and prosperity that the area was built on.

CHAPTER 2

HMCS *Napanee*
K118
Flower Class
Corvette
1939–1940 Program

Photo courtesy Robert F.D. Hall.

HMCS Napanee *now completed, leaving Kingston after grounding in the St. Lawrence River.*

HMCS *NAPANEE* WAS A NEW TYPE OF warship originally classed as escort, whaler type. The type name was changed to corvette by British prime minister Winston Churchill, reviving the old type of ships from the days of sail. She was one of the first of the new corvette design ordered by the Royal Canadian Navy and was constructed to the original specifications. This included a short fo'c'sle (forward deck), main mast before the bridge, second mast aft, short bridge, and minesweeping gear on the stern. She differs greatly in appearance from her sisters HMCS *Belleville* and HMCS *Trentonian*, both revised Flower-class corvettes and constructed later in the war. The intent of her design was to create a ship for multi-tasking, which could serve both as a minesweeper and a coastal convoy escort.

The crew was to be 50 men, which was all that was needed to man and work a ship of this size. Little did the planners realize that by the end of the war these "little ships" would require almost 100 men to operate all the additional equipment installed for the great workload these ships would come to bear. Corvettes have been described many times as the single most uncomfortable and difficult ship for a crew to operate, being well-known as a wet ship and said to "roll on a morning dew." From the beginning of their service, they were moved from the relative shelter of coastal escort to ocean escort, fighting some of the fiercest weather the North Atlantic had to offer.

Napanee was built in Kingston, Ontario, at the Kingston Shipbuilding Yards and assigned the hull number of 17.[1] She was launched on 31 August 1940, and had the honour of being the first corvette to be launched on the Great Lakes. The christening ceremony was performed by Mrs. Angus MacDonald, wife

Photo courtesy of Henry Winsor.

HMCS Napanee *on launch day in Kingston, 31 August 1940.*

of the minister of national defence for naval affairs. The City of Napanee, represented at the ceremony by the mayor and his wife, Dr. and Mrs. Hall, donated and engraved the ship's bell.[2] As Mrs. MacDonald broke the bottle of champagne across *Napanee's* bow, the workman removed the last few blocks from her keel and the ship slid sideways into Lake Ontario.

As soon as the way was clear, another ceremony began. Mr. Angus MacDonald placed the first rivet for the keel of the next corvette to be constructed, while *Napanee* was still bobbing in the water from launching. This marked the first time in the history of the Royal Canadian Navy that a ship was launched and

the keel of the next ship laid in the same day.[3] The new keel belonged to HMCS *Prescott*, who *Napanee* would later serve with on many occasions.

Napanee was the first warship to be ordered by the Royal Canadian Navy from the Kingston yards. By the end of the war, Kingston would build a total of 12 corvettes, two anti-submarine trawlers, and five tugs.

Most of her construction was completed at Kingston, but she was to proceed to Montreal to beat the ice and clear the lakes before winter, as well as to receive her weapons and be completed. *Napanee* departed Kingston on 30 November 1940 in a blinding snowstorm. As she proceeded along the St.

Photo courtesy Henry Winsor.

The crowd watches as HMCS Napanee *is launched sideways into the water. Before she stops bobbing in the water, a new corvette keel is laid in the place where she just left.*

Lawrence River and the Thousand Islands, she had to pass through the Morrisburg Canal. As the ship entered the canal, she ground hard on the bottom, damaging her rudder and propeller, and water poured into the ship from damage to her hull and stern. She was taken in tow and returned to Kingston Shipyards for dry docking and repairs.[4]

Napanee was to be the first corvette commissioned on the Great Lakes, but repairs to the hull took until April 1941, and that honour went instead to HMCS *Collingwood*, built at Collingwood, Ontario.[5]

With the coming of spring, and the ice clear from Lake Ontario, *Napanee* was able to complete her sea trials for acceptance.[6] She was commissioned at Kingston on 12 May 1941, under the command of Lieutenant Commander A.H. Dobson, RCNR.[7] The commissioning ceremony was attended by many citizens of Napanee, including the mayor and his wife.

Immediately following the ceremony, she sailed for Halifax and arrived there on 17 May 1941. Initially she was assigned to the Sydney Force and then later transferred to Newfoundland Command.

A common practice with corvettes was for the crew to paint a portrait on the gun shields of the forward gun to distinguish their ship from others. During the war, new ships were not given an official

Photo courtesy of Henry Winsor.

HMCS Napanee *as she appeared in 1940, still under construction at Kingston, Ontario. Her guns were not yet fitted. She is the first of the ships named for communities on the Bay of Quinte.*

Photo courtesy of Maritime Command Museum, Halifax.

HMCS Napanee *at Kingston, Ontario, on 11 May 1941. Lieutenant Commander Dobson is the tallest officer in the centre of the photo. To his left is Lieutenant Angus, executive officer.*

ship's badge and this informal and personalized "gun-shield art" took its place. *Napanee*'s crew painted the four-inch gun shield with a Native chief wearing a full headdress, devouring a U-boat stern first.[8] The Native imagery was drawn from the popular song "Napanee," written around 1910, with lyrics by W.S Genaro and music by W.R. Williams. The song was about a man in love with a beautiful Native woman named Napanee, and one of the key lyrics is, "my pretty little Napanee."[9]

Napanee joined her first convoy on 18 June 1941, HX 134, consisting of 48 merchant ships,[10] and escorted it as far as Iceland. All convoys were identified with a letter and number designation: "H" was for

Photo courtesy Robert F.D. Hall.

Dr. Duane R. Hall, MD, Mayor of the Town of Napanee, onboard the Flower-class corvette HMCS Napanee *in April 1941.*

Photo courtesy Robert F.D. Hall.

The 4-inch gun of HMCS Napanee *depicting the gun-shield art created by her crew: a Native chief chewing a U-boat.*

Photo courtesy Robert F.D. Hall.

Mrs. Duane R. Hall, Regent, Chapter of the Imperial Daughters of the Empire (IODE), onboard the Flower-class corvette HMCS Napanee, *April 1941.*

Photo courtesy Lennox and Addington County Museum, Napanee. Photographer Geoff Webster.

HMCS Napanee's *gun-shield art on a cloth badge given to her crew.*

Halifax, where the convoy originated, going to the United Kingdom, and "X" stood for fast-travelling convoy, while the number 134 was how many convoys had travelled that particular route. At this early point of the war, escort ships were in high demand, and as soon as the ships were built and commissioned they were immediately set to work. This left the crews with little time to train or learn the equipment in their new ship — most training was "on the job" and in some cases trial by fire, as inexperienced crews had to fight a highly trained and professional enemy.

On 24 September 1941, *Napanee* escorted SC 46 with corvettes *Lethbridge* and *Shediac* and destroyers *Ottawa* and *St. Croix*.[11] "SC" is the designation for a slow convoy from Sydney or Halifax, Nova Scotia, or New York City, to the United Kingdom. HMCS *St. Croix* was the Senior Officer (SO) of the escort group, the highest ranking or most senior commanding officer in the group, and he was responsible for commanding the escort group as well as his own ship. The convoy was large, with 53 merchant ships leaving from Sydney, Cape Breton. Initially, the weather consisted of rain squalls and heavy fog, making the intended route through the Strait of Belle Isle more difficult. This narrow strait that separates Newfoundland from Labrador is treacherous in the best of weather and seldom used in peacetime. In war it offered some

inshore protection to convoys before they headed out to the open North Atlantic.

By midday of the 26th, the fog had become dense and visibility very poor. *Napanee*'s lookouts spotted a merchant ship in the fog steaming the wrong way, toward the Labrador coast. Dobson ordered the ship about and tried to signal the merchant ship, but it disappeared back into the fog, and a second ship was spotted right behind the first. Dobson ordered *Napanee* to close with the freighter and this time a signal was passed to the merchant ship and the freighter was able to steer clear. The senior officer of the escort group in *St. Croix* radioed *Napanee* that an unknown number of merchant ships had run aground on the north shore, so Dobson ordered the ship away from the convoy and headed back toward the Labrador coast. At least five ships had run aground and one, *Empire Mallard*, had already foundered. Dobson tried to pass a line from *Napanee* to the

DND MC-2683. Photo courtesy Archives and Collections Society, Picton.

Her pendant number has been removed by censors; Napanee's gun-shield art is clearly visible on her forward gun. This picture demonstrates the size of a corvette compared to the merchant ships they are to protect.

grounded freighter *Culebra* but was unsuccessful due to the rising seas. He then radioed Sydney for a salvage tug. As the storm increased, *Napanee* could only stand by the stricken ship, unable to offer any assistance. In the dark, they lost contact with the freighter and feared the ship could be sinking and the men in her dying. *Napanee* was helpless to save them.

As dawn began to shed some light, *Culebra* could be seen again, still on the rocks and in one piece. *Napanee* closed the freighter again and Dobson signalled his intention to pass a line to tow the freighter off the rocks. The master of the freighter refused, stating he was worried his ship would sink if pulled off the rocks, and would wait for the tug. *Napanee* then joined with *Lethbridge* and proceeded to Forteau Bay to rescue other survivors from the night before. But still the heavy seas made rescue impossible and *Napanee* was ordered back to Sydney.

Dobson was frustrated that he couldn't do more. His superiors felt just the opposite: that night *Napanee* saved many ships from grounding and managed to turn the convoy away from danger.

On 29 September 1941, *Napanee* left Sydney with convoy SC 47, escorting it as far as Iceland. The convoy consisted of 63 ships and travelled at the grand speed of seven knots, arriving safely at Liverpool on 20 October 1941 after an uneventful crossing. It was lucky; the next convoy that left Sydney, a week later, lost nine of 52 ships to German submarine wolf packs.[12]

In November, Lieutenant Commander Dobson received a signal from Naval Headquarters in Ottawa: "The Department notes with satisfaction a report from NOIC (Naval Officer in Charge) Sydney that 'great credit is due to HMCS *Napanee*,' A/Lieut.-Commander A.H. Dobson, RCNR, for warning a number of ships

[of SC 46] of the danger into which they were steaming and successfully leading them out of it."

In recognition of his seamanship, leadership, and command skills, Dobson was transferred from *Napanee* and placed in command of a four-stack destroyer, HMCS *St. Croix*, on loan to the RCN from the United States, and made senior officer of the escort group.[13] Command of *Napanee* passed to Lieutenant S. Henderson, RCNR, on 9 December 1941.

In January 1942, *Napanee* started out on her first of many "Newfie-Derry" runs. The route was given this nickname because the escort groups sailed from Newfoundland to Londonderry. In preparation for her next convoy, *Napanee* was to draw fuel from the oil tanker SS *Thunder*. She ended up grounding briefly when she started to drift away from the tanker. Lieutenant Henderson ordered both anchors dropped to stop the ship from drifting onto the shore, and while the windlass to lower the anchors was kept clear of ice and running, the anchors were fouled with ice and remained in place. A slight shudder was felt throughout the ship and the anti-submarine officer immediately reported to the bridge, "Dome Damaged or Gone." A tug was brought in to free *Napanee* and secure her to another tanker, SS *Teakwood*.[14]

This delayed *Napanee* from joining her first Newfie-Derry convoy. After repairs she eventually left to join convoy SC 65, which departed from Halifax on 17 January 1942 with 36 ships and arrived in Liverpool on 4 February 1942 without incident.

From 20 May to 20 July 1942, *Napanee* was in refit at Liverpool, Nova Scotia. At this time, her after mast was removed and a Radio Direction Finder (RDF) was installed. She did not undergo the major structural changes that most early corvettes would be given until her next refit.[15]

DND MC-2681, Photo courtesy Archives and Collections Society Picton.

HMCS Napanee *showing the changes made after her first refit in June 1942. The most obvious are that her after mast has been removed and her radar has been fitted aft of the bridge.*

During the summer, *Napanee* was given the task of escorting an Admiralty tug. The tug would leave St. John's Harbour and go 1,000 miles or so into the Atlantic to tow in a damaged or disabled freighter.[16] The ship made three consecutive trips like this, and it was a total of six weeks before her crew touched shore again.

On 8 August 1942, *Napanee* left St. John's to escort the damaged destroyer HMCS *Assiniboine*,[17] which had been in close action with the German submarine *U-210*. *Assiniboine* had found the submarine on the surface, and a running battle ensued.

The destroyer and submarine were so close together that *Assiniboine* couldn't use her 4.7-inch guns and had to fire at the submarine with only her machine guns. The submarine, being smaller, was able to fire her 37-millimetre gun directly at the destroyer, scoring several hits and starting a fire outside the wheelhouse. Eventually, *Assiniboine* was able to open the distance and scored a direct hit on the submarine's conning tower, killing the German skipper. *U-210* then attempted to dive, but *Assiniboine* rammed her aft of the conning tower. Seeing that the U-boat was still attempting to escape, *Assiniboine* rammed her a second time. This time the submarine was finished: the crew abandoned ship and the submarine sank in two minutes. *Assiniboine* was severely damaged during the encounter, and *Napanee* escorted the destroyer first to Newfoundland then to Halifax for repairs.

Later that month, on 26 August 1942, *Napanee* located a ditched Walrus patrol aircraft off Sable Island.[18] The float plane was unable to fly but still afloat and was taken in tow, heading to Sydney, Nova Scotia. Unfortunately, the aircraft could not stand up to being towed on the open ocean, and after two days was lost.[19]

On 5 September 1942, *Napanee* and the rest of the 1st Canadian Escort Group (C1) departed Halifax with convoy SC 99.[20] It consisted of 59 ships, and the other escorts were the destroyer HMCS *St. Francis*, an old four-stacker on loan from the United States Navy; and the corvettes *Battleford, Chambly, Chilliwack, Eyebright, Orillia,* and *Rosthern.* The enemy sighted the convoy on 13 September 1942, and it was closed by five U-boats. The wolf pack was drawn off when they were ordered to close with convoy ON 129 and no attack was made on SC 99.[21] Most of *Napanee's* escort duties were performed with little or no problems along the way, but their luck was about to run out.

On 19 December 1942, *Napanee* and her escort group departed Liverpool with convoy ONS 154[22] to New York City. This was to be a slow convoy and they would be entering the "Black Pit" around Christmas Day — it would be after New Year's Day before they

HMCS Napanee, *outboard with signal flags, in harbour with two unidentified corvettes.*

DND MC-2685, Photo courtesy Archives and Collections Society, Picton.

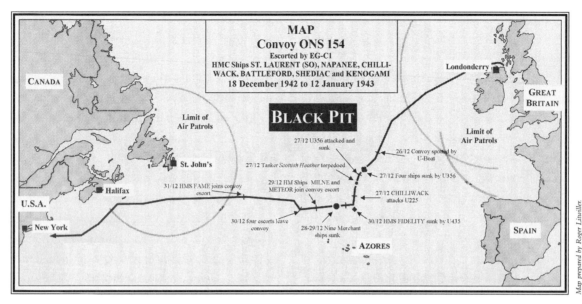

Map showing the route of convoy ONS 154 from England to New York City.

would sail out of it. The Black Pit was the area of the Atlantic Ocean where convoys were out of range of air cover, and was the hunting ground of the German submarine wolf packs. What the convoy and escort ships couldn't know was that one of the greatest convoy battles of the Second World War was about to begin.

Convoy ONS 154 departed British waters at the tail end of a hurricane. The escort group was entirely Canadian and consisted of the destroyer HMCS *St. Laurent*, as senior officer in command of the escort group, followed by the corvettes *Napanee*, *Shediac*, *Kenogami*, *Chilliwack*, and *Battleford*. A second destroyer, HMS *Burwell*, an old four-stacker, was unable to join them, due to defects and breakdowns. She was not replaced, so escort group C1 left with one destroyer missing. The reduction in the number of escorts left the convoy with less protection overall; the loss of a destroyer, with its relative speed

and manoeuvrability, especially hindered the escort group's ability to hunt down U-boats.

The convoy itself consisted of 46 merchant ships; this included a rescue ship, SS *Toward*, and a "special service ship," HMS *Fidelity*. *Fidelity* was equipped with High Frequency Direction Finder (HF/DF), asdic (sonar),[23] two Grumman seaplanes, and a Motor Torpedo Boat (MTB). The unusual vessel was an old coal-burning merchant ship with a maximum speed of 12 knots. She was on passage to the Far East, and unfortunately the presence and capabilities of this ship were not passed on to the escort commander in *St. Laurent*.

The convoy travelled at a speed of seven knots. The merchant ships were organized in 12 columns, forming a rectangle six miles wide and two miles deep. The convoy's track was moved south of the normal route to avoid a line of known U-boats and allow 18

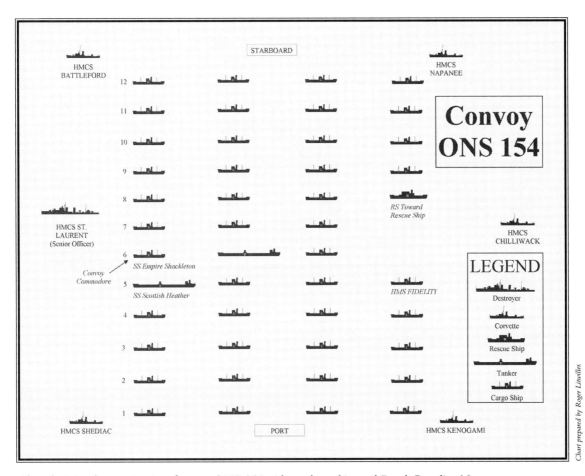

HMCS
BATTLEFORD

STARBOARD

HMCS
NAPANEE

Convoy ONS 154

HMCS ST.
LAURENT
(Senior Officer)

RS Toward
Rescue Ship

HMCS
CHILLIWACK

Convoy
Commodore

SS Empire Shackleton

SS Scottish Heather

HMS FIDELITY

LEGEND

Destroyer

Corvette

Rescue Ship

Tanker

Cargo Ship

HMCS SHEDIAC

PORT

HMCS KENOGAMI

Chart prepared by Roger Litwiller.

Chart depicting the organization of convoy ONS 154 with merchant ships and Royal Canadian Navy escorts.

ships bound for the South Atlantic to be detached near the Azores. This would require the convoy to remain in the Black Pit longer than was typical.

The escorts and merchant ships fought the high seas and winds from the remnants of the hurricane. Most of the merchant ships were empty and riding high in the water, making it difficult to keep station in the convoy, so the escorts used a large quantity of fuel while shepherding the merchant ships back into their respective lines and finding stragglers.

Napanee was in need of fuel and was detailed to the convoy's fuel ship, the tanker SS *Scottish Heather*. Refuelling the escorts at sea was then fairly experimental and a precarious task at the best of times; add to this inherent difficulty the movement of two ships underway, attempting to match and maintain speed and course while responding to the waves, wind, and sea. With great difficulty, the fuel hose was finally brought aboard the corvette, and to everyone's dismay the threads on the hose did not match the fuel standpipe on the ship. The access hatches to the fuel tanks were removed and the hose fed directly into the tanks. This required almost the entire off-watch crew to maintain the hose, as the ships would spread apart and veer together as they moved through the waves. It was a dirty and sloppy job, prone to spills of the thick bunker oil.

The convoy sailed westward and finally, as planned, crossed into the Black Pit on Christmas Day, when someone pencilled in "Merry Christmas" across the top of *Napanee*'s log.

The first enemy contact with the convoy was during the night of 26 December by German submarine *U-664*; she transmitted a convoy sighting report. *Shediac*, stationed on the port bow of the convoy, followed a radar contact and found *U-664* on the surface. In order to illuminate the submarine, *Shediac* fired starshell, forcing it to crash dive and lose contact with the convoy. But with tensions high, the ships of the convoy continued to illuminate the sky, the escort ships firing starshell and the merchant ships a smaller version called snowflake, for over an hour. Unfortunately, each bright flare in the sky served as a beacon, calling to nearby submarines.

Starboard-side view of Napanee *post-refit.*

CN-3805, Photo courtesy National Defence Imaging Library.

Early in the morning of the 27th, *U-356* gained visual contact with the convoy and transmitted a sighting report. This time *St. Laurent* followed a HF/DF bearing from SS *Toward* and gained a fleeting radar contact of the submarine, but was unable to get a visual or asdic sighting. The opening shots of the battle were made by *U-411* at 0213 as she fired torpedoes at three different ships on the starboard bow of the convoy, though none found their target. The convoy then made a prearranged course-change to the southwest, but this put *U-356* in a good firing position on the starboard side of the convoy, and at 0240 first blood was drawn. The submarine fired her torpedoes and hit the lead ships in the 10th and 12th columns; SS *Melrose, Abbey* (II), and SS *Empire Union* were sunk with 13 dead. The convoy commander ordered a search for the unseen enemy, but the submarine remained hidden, and *Napanee* was ordered to screen the rescue ship *Toward* as she picked up survivors at the rear of the convoy.

Shortly after, at 0300, *St. Laurent* gained another radar contact and pursued it. At 0310 *U-356* closed the convoy again and torpedoed the Dutch freighter SS *Soekaboemi*, at the rear of the 11th column. The ship remained afloat and the crew escaped in lifeboats, with one dead. Five minutes later *U-356* torpedoed the freighter SS *King Edward* at the head of the eighth column, with the loss of 23 lives. *St. Laurent* found *U-411* on the surface and forced her down at 0352, following up with several depth charge attacks.

The battle now shifted to *Napanee*'s location in the convoy: *U-356* was spotted at 0530 on the surface, trimmed down and approaching the starboard quarter of the convoy for another attack. *St. Laurent* raced in and registered several hits on the conning tower with her Oerlikon machine guns before the submarine dived. The destroyer raced in and dropped a pattern of five depth charges at the location where *U-356* had submerged and then opened the range to 1,300 yards to regain asdic contact and hunt it down. Contact was regained and the asdic operator heard a roar from below, sounding as though the submarine were blowing tanks to dive farther. A second attack was made on the sub; this time the depth charges were set from 50 to 140 feet and a pattern of 10 were dropped. The asdic operator counted 11 explosions, the last was delayed and intense. A third attack was made and this produced a large oil slick on the surface, but no wreckage. Contact with the submarine was lost after the escort group's last attack at 0600.

Napanee continued to screen the rescue ship *Toward* as she picked up 170 merchant sailors from the four torpedoed ships — *Napanee* herself rescued 25 men from *King Edward* and 18 from *Soekaboemi*. The rescue operations lasted until dawn, and *Soekaboemi* was the only one of the four to remain afloat, though damaged. She was left behind to make the safety of port on her own. *U-411* resurfaced at 0914, and, finding herself in the vicinity of the stricken ship, she shadowed her most of that day until finally sinking her that evening. *U-411* had one diesel engine out of service and could not make contact with the convoy again, so she withdrew from the battle.

As the next evening was approaching, the situation was still very grave. The Admiralty confirmed at least four U-boats were in contact with the convoy and another six were approaching. Western Approaches Command ordered the convoy to alter course to the south and looked in vain for escorts to divert to ONS 154 to assist. The closest available were the British destroyers HMS *Milne* and *Meteor*, two full days away. Desperate, the senior officer of the escorts,

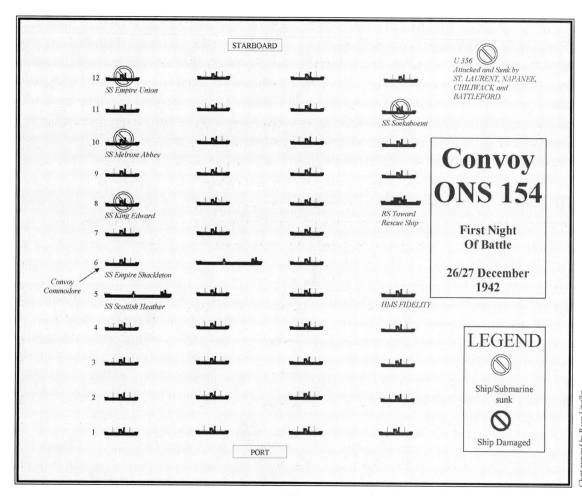

Convoy and German losses following the first night of the battle.

in *St. Laurent*, made false radio calls to fictitious escorts in an attempt to trick the growing wolf pack into believing that more ships were nearby. The ruse was ineffective as five more U-boats joined the pack in the afternoon, guided by sighting reports from *U-225*.

As evening set, the escorts were in need of fuel, and the tanker SS *Scottish Heather* was detailed to refuel *Chilliwack* astern of the convoy. With great difficulty the fuel hose was passed from the tanker to

the corvette and again the hose could not be fitted to the standpipe. The tanker started pumping the thick bunker oil to *Chilliwack*, and barely one ton of fuel had been transferred when *Scottish Heather* exploded.

The two ships had been found by *U-225* at their most vulnerable moment. The submarine took up station to attack the tanker in the hopes that the resulting inferno would serve as a great beacon upon the water. At 2030 *U-225* fired her torpedoes, and although the tanker was hit, the fuel she was carrying did not catch fire, foiling the U-boat's plan. *Chilliwack* sighted the submarine and immediately ran in for the attack, firing her Oerlikons at the surfaced sub. *U-225* made a crash dive and stayed down, losing contact with the convoy. *Scottish Heather*, damaged, was able to limp back to port, but the convoy escorts had now lost their fuel source, and fuel was running low.

As midnight approached, a merchant ship near *Napanee* fired a starshell, and a silhouette appeared directly ahead of her. While this silhouette was first thought to be another escort, it turned out to be a U-boat on the surface, facing the convoy. The skipper ordered full ahead to ram and the 4-inch gun fired starshell above as the sub crash dived. As *Napanee* passed the location where the U-boat disappeared, a full pattern of depth charges were dropped and the corvette opened the distance to 1,000 yards to regain contact and set up another attack. The second attack produced a huge bubble on the surface, but *Napanee* was ordered to rejoin the convoy and was therefore unable to pursue the contact or confirm a kill.

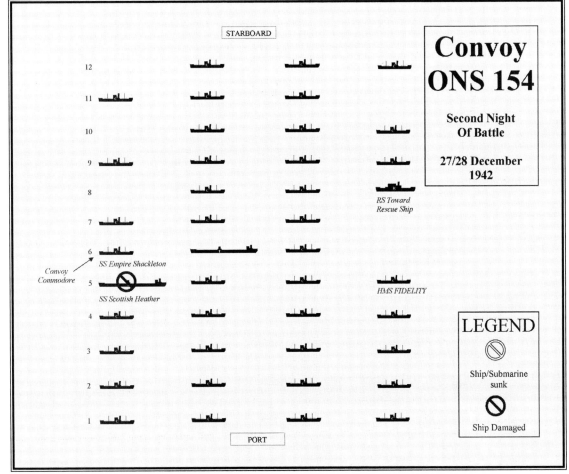

STARBOARD

Convoy ONS 154

Second Night Of Battle

27/28 December 1942

12
11
10
9
8

RS Toward Rescue Ship

7
6

SS Empire Shackleton

Convoy Commodore

5

SS Scottish Heather

HMS FIDELITY

4

LEGEND

Ship/Submarine sunk

Ship Damaged

3
2
1

PORT

Chart prepared by Roger Litwiller.

Convoy losses following the second night of the battle.

During the night, the weather started to deteriorate, fog and mist were moving in, and the seas were increasing. This was good for the convoy, and the only U-boat to remain in contact was *U-260,* who had sighted an escort at 0013. The submarine used his *Metox*, an early German radar detector, to keep station with the convoy and for seven hours sent reports and beacons to the other U-boats, preventing ONS 154 from escaping.

At 0225 on 28 December, *St. Laurent* gained another radar contact, *U-615.* They could not make a visual or asdic contact until 15 minutes later when the destroyer regained the radar contact, made a visual sighting, and raced in at 25 knots to attack. *U-615* dived and *St. Laurent* dropped her depth charges on the location where the sub went down. The skipper adopted the same tactic he had used the night before on *U-356* and made a series of attacks. This time the attacks produced a large oil slick on the surface, and the skipper radioed to Western Approaches, "Got him, dropped 10 charges heard 14 explosions one enormous." Despite the escort commander's

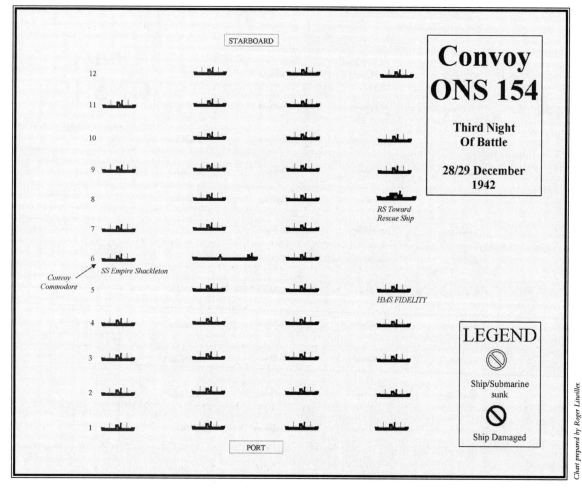

Convoy ONS 154

Third Night
Of Battle

28/29 December
1942

STARBOARD

RS Toward
Rescue Ship

SS Empire Shackleton

Convoy
Commodore

HMS FIDELITY

LEGEND

Ship/Submarine
sunk

Ship Damaged

PORT

Chart prepared by Roger Litwiller.

Convoy losses following the third night of the battle.

claim of victory, *U-615* made her escape undamaged. As the fog and visibility worsened, no other attacks were made the rest of the night by either side. This gave the escorts and convoy a reprieve and a chance to prepare for the battle that was coming. The radio signals from the German submarines were still being picked up by the HF/DF, but again no sightings or attacks were made.

By the next morning, the 29th, the Admiralty reported six enemy submarines were in direct contact with the convoy and an additional 12 were joining. The Germans would soon outnumber the escorts by a factor of three to one. The convoy was ordered to alter course to the west, in the hope of still avoiding the concentration of U-boats, but several submarines were able to gain glimpses of the convoy through the fog and remain in contact.

The poor weather and visibility that had protected the convoy for the last day and a half suddenly lifted. As the sky cleared, eight submarines had direct visual contact of the convoy. The U-boats remained on the surface just outside of the escorts' attack range, openly hunting the convoy as a pack of wolves stalks a deer, knowing their prey can no longer escape. Their numbers continued to grow, and just before sunset 11 submarines were surfaced on both sides of the convoy, about five miles away. The senior officer in *St. Laurent* urged HMS *Fidelity* to launch one of her seaplanes to assist with the evening course-change and drive off some of the U-boats. But, as the waves continued to grow, the seaplane crashed on takeoff into a 12-foot wave. Fortunately *St. Laurent* was able to rescue the two-man aircrew.

The men of the convoy took to the decks, lifebelts inflated and fearful of being trapped below decks, knowing that a deadly attack was now inevitable.

They did not have to wait long. As the sun set, the sky and the ocean combined into a blackness that the eye could not penetrate. The first attack came at 1941 when *U-203* and *U-435* each made separate unsuccessful attacks on ONS 154.

Just before the moon was to rise, *Battleford* gained a radar contact and closed to investigate. What she found was astounding: four U-boats on the surface in line-ahead formation, bearing down on the convoy for attack and using light signals to co-ordinate themselves as they raced in. *Battleford* illuminated the attacking U-boats and opened fire with assistance from *Chilliwack*, successfully breaking up the first concentrated attempt by the submarines to penetrate the convoy. But it cost *Battleford* her radar, as it was knocked out of service by the blast of her own guns.

Chilliwack then found *U-615* on the port bow and attacked, forcing the submarine out of the battle. In the meantime, *St. Laurent* was returning to the convoy from rescuing the downed aircrew, and as she approached the convoy from the rear she spotted a U-boat on the surface at 2008. She and *Kenogami* drove in for the attack, forcing the submarine to submerge; neither ship gained an asdic contact, but both dropped depth charges where the sub was last seen. A few minutes later, *Napanee* held a solid asdic contact on the starboard quarter of the convoy. She illuminated the area, found a U-boat on the surface, and forced the submarine under.

The attacks stopped as suddenly as they began, and at 2045 the senior officer in *St. Laurent* radioed to Western Approaches Command, "Attack repulsed. No ships torpedoed. Every escort has had a fight. Some promising attacks were made." The message was correct; 10 of the 11 U-boats in contact with the convoy had been forced from the battle or driven down. Unknown to the senior officer, the battle was only just beginning — the convoy was heading into a pack of 13 more submarines.

The events earlier had left the escorts disorganized: *Shediac* was escorting HMS *Fidelity*, still astern of the convoy after the unsuccessful attempt to launch her floatplane; *Battleford* did not know of the convoy's course-change and became separated, unable to locate the convoy without her radar until the next morning. This left only four escorts with the convoy and the starboard bow and port beam of the convoy open to the U-boats' attack.

U-591 found herself in this perfect firing position created by the unprotected starboard bow of the convoy, and the U-boat fired her torpedoes at

2052, hitting SS *Norse King*, who was carrying 5,400 tons of coal. A few minutes later, *Napanee* avoided another barrage of torpedoes, possibly fired from the same submarine. *Napanee*'s lookouts reported two surfaced U-boats, but starshell illuminated only a possible wake and no visual contact was gained. At 2102, *U-225* fired a spread of four torpedoes, also from the starboard bow of the convoy. The submarine came under heavy machine-gun fire and crash dived, though the torpedoes found their target and two more merchant ships were hit in the 11th column, SS *Melmore Head* in ballast and SS *Ville de Rouen* with 5,500 tons general cargo.

Also at this time, *St. Laurent,* astern of the convoy, and *Chilliwack,* on the port bow, attacked and thought they had sunk submarines. At some point

HMCS Napanee's *bow lifting clear of the water in a moderate sea.*

DND MC-2682. Photo courtesy Archives and Collections Society Picton.

during the battle, *Chilliwack* lost her radar and was damaged by an explosion from one of her own depth charges. The senior officer in *St. Laurent* became aware of the missing *Battleford* and moved up to cover the starboard bow of the convoy. An alteration in the convoy's course to the west placed *U-260* directly ahead. The U-boat fired her torpedoes at 2127, hitting the only remaining ship of the 11th column. SS *Empire Wagtail*, carrying a full load of coal, exploded instantly and was lost with all 43 of her crew.

The low clouds over the convoy were lit up by starshell from the escorts and snowflake from the merchant ships. *U-406* used the light to position herself for another attack; she was carrying the new FAT torpedoes. These were a pattern-running torpedo and had an accuracy rating of 75 percent. The U-boat fired her four torpedoes at 2217 and struck three merchant ships on the port side of the convoy in the first and second columns: *Baron Cochrane*, carrying 3,000 tons of coal; *Lynton Grange*, with almost 6,000 tons of general cargo; and *Zarian*, with 7,500 tons of general cargo. *U-406* withdrew from the port side of the convoy and later crash dived to avoid an escort. She was not detected due to the lost radar on both *Chilliwack* and *Kenogami*.

At this point the defence of the convoy started to break down as the senior officer in *St. Laurent* ordered the escorts to fire starshell independently. The night sky above the convoy was illuminated by starshell from the escorts and snowflake from the merchant ships, giving clear visibility of the convoy to the wolf pack and not revealing the U-boats. At the same time, the ocean itself was filled with tracer fire: white from the merchant ships and escorts, and pink from the attacking submarines. The torpedoes were so numerous that the officer of the watch in

Shediac reported to the skipper, "There goes our one now!" as if acknowledging a passing taxi instead of a deadly torpedo. The battle for ONS 154 had become an all-out brawl.

The commanding officer of *U-225* now worked his way back to the head of the convoy, torpedoes reloaded since his last attack two hours before. The U-boat entered the convoy and fired five torpedoes, hitting the convoy commodore's ship at the head of the sixth column, *Empire Shackelton*, carrying a mixed load of cargo and ammunition, and the tanker *President Francqui,* just astern. *Napanee*'s skipper remarked that the convoy had become "a holocaust." Lieutenant Henderson would later write, "All ships appeared to be firing snowflakes, and tracers crisscrossed in all directions, escorts firing starshell. The sea was dotted with lights from boats and rafts and two burning wrecks which had hauled out to starboard helped the illumination."

Two merchant ships had moved aside of the convoy and were burning fiercely, while six more merchant ships now lay astern of the convoy, damaged and helpless. The crippled merchant ships were then finished off by the U-boats one by one.

The attack by the wolf pack now diminished as some of the U-boats had become low on fuel and torpedoes and were ordered to locate and sink the stragglers. Three submarines now remained in contact with the convoy, but no further attacks were recorded. ONS 154 was the victim of the most successful attack by a wolf pack of the Battle of the Atlantic; six submarines had sunk nine ships in just two hours.

During the day of the 30th, two submerged attacks were attempted against the convoy without success. The escorts were reinforced during the day as the two destroyers sent to their aid, HMS *Milne* and

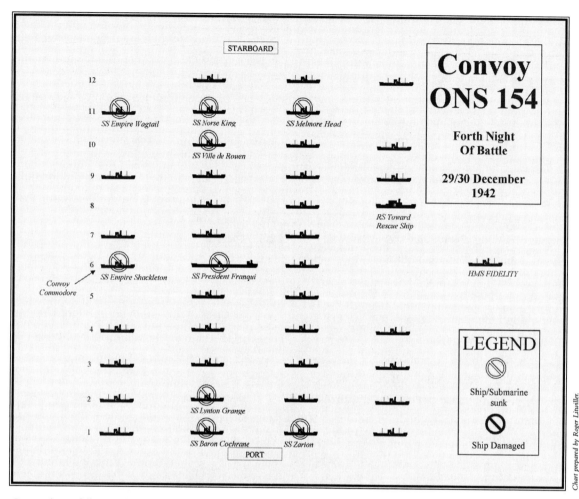

Convoy losses following the fourth night of the battle.

HMS *Meteor*, finally joined the convoy. At the same time, two more submarines joined the three U-boats shadowing the convoy. That night, *Milne* and *Meteor* attacked several HF/DF contacts and there were no successful U-boat attacks that night.

HMS *Fidelity*, still behind the convoy following her unsuccessful launch of a seaplane and unable to retake the convoy due to engine problems, proceeded to the Azores independently. For her own defence she still had asdic, HF/DF, a motor torpedo boat, and one seaplane remaining.

She was pursued by *U-225*, *U-665*, *U-615*, and *U-435* as she made her way to the Azores, but was able to successfully use her seaplane to force two of the submarines to crash dive and lose contact, and her torpedo boat interfered with *U-615*'s attack. Her luck ran out on the 30th when *U-435* attacked and sank her, taking 374 lives including Vice-Admiral Egerton

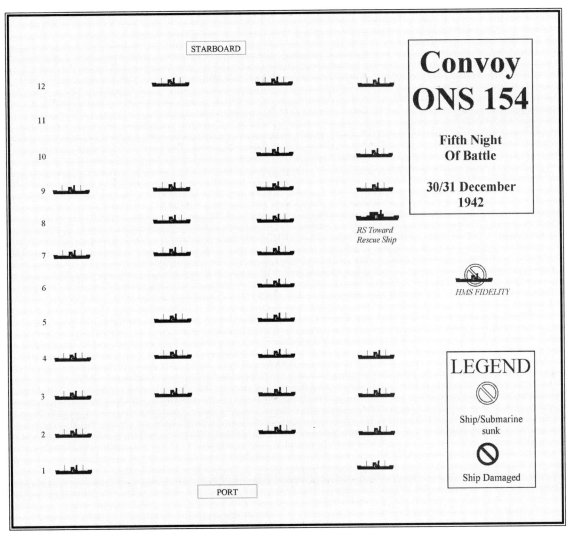

STARBOARD

12
11
10
9
8
7
6
5
4
3
2
1

**Convoy
ONS 154**

**Fifth Night
Of Battle**

**30/31 December
1942**

*RS Toward
Rescue Ship*

HMS FIDELITY

LEGEND

Ship/Submarine
sunk

Ship Damaged

PORT

Chart prepared by Roger Litwiller.

Convoy losses following the fifth night of the battle.

and the other survivors from the *Empire Shackleton*. HMS *Fidelity*'s torpedo boat survived the attack and, with the few survivors aboard, started to make her way independently back to the U.K. — until she ran out of fuel. She was later found by HMCS *Woodstock*, proceeding under a makeshift sail. After rescuing the crew, *Woodstock* sank the torpedo boat by gunfire.

That same afternoon, *Shediac* and *Battleford* were detached from the escort due to low fuel and headed for the Azores. HMS *Milne* and *Meteor* were also low on fuel and sent off. Both destroyers had consumed a large quantity of fuel in the rush to reinforce the convoy, arrived after the big battle, and now were forced to leave before the convoy left the Black Pit.

The convoy was more vulnerable now than during the entire battle, with only four of the escorts remaining: *St. Laurent* and *Napanee*, battle-weary and still in fighting shape, *Kenogami* and *Chilliwack*, both without radar and the latter damaged from one of her own depth charges earlier in the battle.

It was at this point that the senior officer ordered the convoy, if the opportunity arose, to make independently for safety. This was as near as an admission of total defeat as was possible, and meant that the escort was no longer in a position to protect the convoy.

The four escort ships that had left the convoy for the Azores the day before had their own problems to overcome. *Shediac* had to be towed the last 40 miles to port by *Battleford* when she ran out of fuel, and HMS *Milne* towed the last five miles by HMS *Meteor*.

On 31 December 1942, the sea was increasing and the submarines were finding it difficult to maintain a sighting of ONS 154. The last contact made was at 1652 by *U-455*, but the other U-boats had continued on an incorrect heading and were too far away to regain contact. The escort group was reinforced by the British destroyer HMS *Fame,* who took over as senior officer of the escort. By this time, the senior officer in *St. Laurent* had succumbed to the anguish and fatigue of five days of continuous battle and had to be relieved, command of his ship going to the executive officer.

The convoy reached New York City on 1 January 1943, without the usual celebrations of New Year's Day. The battered escort group reached St. John's Harbour on 4 January 1943. Even though the battle for convoy ONS 154 was behind them, *Napanee* still had one last minor misfortune ahead of her. She landed survivors from the convoy on the north side of St. John's Harbour and proceeded for

fuel. At the time, the harbour was particularly congested and it was necessary for *Napanee* to steam to the western end to turn and approach the tanker SS *Teakwood*. When *Napanee* was abreast of the tanker, her starboard anchor was dropped to swing alongside. As the two ships came together, *Napanee's* port anchor bumped the side of *Teakwood*, causing a slight dent in the tanker's side and damaging a stanchion. *Napanee* was undamaged, but the investigation later found her skipper at fault for not approaching at the right angle. No disciplinary action was taken.[24]

The battle for ONS 154 had been monumental: 46 merchant ships, escorted by one Canadian destroyer and five corvettes, later reinforced by three British destroyers, faced a total of 21 German U-boats from three separate wolf packs. At times the escort group was outnumbered four to one. These were impossible odds when there was no air cover to assist in the protection of the convoy. By the final tally, 13 merchant ships had been sunk, one more damaged, and one Royal Navy ship, HMS *Fidelity*, sunk. All told, 551 Royal Navy and Allied merchant sailors lost their lives, 564 sailors were rescued, and one, the captain of SS *President Franqui*, was taken prisoner by *U-336*. The Germans lost one submarine and its crew of 46 sailors. It wasn't until after the war that *Napanee*, *St. Laurent*, *Chilliwack*, and *Battleford* were given equal credit for sinking *U-356* during the first night of the battle.

The fallout from the attack on convoy ONS 154 was extensive: the British Admiralty used this event as their prime example of why the Royal Canadian Navy was unable to perform their duties as a whole and barred the RCN from the North Atlantic, citing poor equipment, manpower, and training. To overcome this, the RCN was sent back to school.

ONS 154 was not the only reason for this decision; it was based on several unsuccessful convoy battles. The RCN did suffer severely from the deficiencies cited by the British Admiralty. To provide some perspective on the reasons for the lack of equipment, training, and experience of the sailors, consider that Canada entered the war in 1939 with six destroyers and 2,000 men. The Canadian Navy was given the task of escorting the convoys to and from England. To accomplish this, the navy had to expand by a ratio of 50 to one; for every one sailor at the beginning of the war, 50 had to be trained. Also, the new technology to fight submarines, radar and sonar, along with the new weapons, were all British-designed and built. The Royal Navy made sure all of its ships received this new equipment first, before it was installed into the RCN ships. Therefore, the RCN ships were expected to perform the same jobs as their RN counterparts with old and outdated equipment. The Royal Navy's decision to remove the RCN from the North Atlantic was eventually resolved, and the RCN went on to command the North Atlantic, ending the war with the third largest navy of all combatants. To fight these enemy ships, we had over 100,000 men and women proudly wearing the naval uniform.

At the end of February 1943, escort group C1 was sent for training at HMS *Western Isles*, the Royal Navy training base at Tobermory, Scotland. The training commander was Commodore G. Stephenson, also known as the "Terror of Tobermory." His training method became legendary as he inspired and terrorized escort captains and their crews.

Napanee and escort group C1 were not spared the attention of the commodore as they spent six days of continuous workups and evolutions. They performed anti-submarine sweeps, gunnery practice, boarding party tactics, depth charge attacks, anti-aircraft defence, and graduation itself was an intensive night-fighting exercise.

Napanee was not assigned to Operation Torch, the planned invasion of North Africa, but did escort one convoy as far as Gibraltar in support of the invasion. *Napanee* made the trip with escort group C1, leaving Londonderry on 27 February 1943. The convoy was KMS 10,[25] 57 merchant ships escorted by HMCS *St. Croix*, *Napanee*, *Battleford*, *Kenogami*, and *Shediac*.[26] Also in company was the RN's 16th Minesweeping Flotilla, consisting of *Fort York*, *Parrsboro*, *Qualicum*, and *Wedgeport*. The escort group was placed under temporary command of the senior officer in the RN destroyer HMS *Burwell*. This increase in escorts for the Gibraltar convoys was due to the constant danger of attack from the U-boats and the added attacks of German shore-based aircraft.

The first attack on KMS 10 came on 4 March 1943, when two German Kondor aircraft attacked from the west, about 250 miles from Cape St. Vincent. The anti-aircraft fire from the escorts and merchant ships repelled the planes. One of the aircraft then made a solo attack on the Catalina patrol aircraft flying astern of the convoy. Several hits were observed on the German aircraft.

The Kondors were always a prelude to the U-boats. The aircraft would find the convoy and the submarines would then be "homed in." This attack was no exception. *Shediac* detected *U-87* at 1240 on 4 March 1943, six miles astern of the convoy. The corvette immediately made a series of five attacks on the submarine, dropping 38 depth charges, and *St. Croix* joined the attack at 1400. *Shediac* made two more attacks and a large amount of oil was produced on the surface. The asdic operators heard the sound of a submarine blowing tanks to surface and the crew cheered as they waited for the U-boat to appear. When she failed to surface, *St. Croix* made two more attacks on dubious contacts. At 1510 both ships broke off the attack and returned to the convoy. The submarine had indeed been sunk, probably having tried to make an attempt to surface but failing and sinking into the depths.

German aircraft continued to shadow KMS 10 and on 6 March 1943 three submarines made contact. The first successful attack against the convoy came at 1418 when *U-410* torpedoed *Fort Paskoyac* on the starboard side. One minute later, *Fort Battle River*, carrying 3,000 tons of stores, was torpedoed by the same U-boat on the port side and later sank. *St. Croix* and *Napanee* carried out a search for the U-boat, and *St. Croix* attacked a firm contact with no obvious results. The two ships then returned to the convoy. *Napanee's* escort group was relieved by the Gibraltar force on 7 March 1943 and proceeded to escort the convoy to its destination of Bone, Algeria.

Napanee and the rest of escort group C1 were given just 24 hours in Gibraltar. This gave the crews very little time to fuel and re-ammunition the ships, but there was time for a quick run ashore.

The escort group returned to England with convoy MKS 9 on 8 March 1943.[27] This convoy of 55 merchant ships was similarly shadowed by aircraft and also came under attack from U-boats. On 13 March 1943, *U-163* was detected by HMCS *Prescott*, who made several attacks. She was eventually joined by *Napanee* and *Baddeck* in search of the submarine, and later *Prescott* made a further attack on a solid asdic contact at 2319, firing a nine-depth-charge pattern. She remained in the area for three more hours while the other ships rejoined the convoy. *Napanee* and *Prescott* share the credit for the sinking of *U-163*.[28] The convoy arrived back in England on 14 March 1943 without any losses.

CN-3549, Photo courtesy National Defence Imaging Library.

HMCS Napanee *toward the end of her refit in Montreal, during the summer of 1943.*

Following the side trip south, *Napanee*, with escort group C1, returned to her old duties on the North Atlantic, rejoining the Newfie-Derry run on 29 March, escorting convoy ONS 2. This was a convoy of 31 merchant ships from Londonderry to Halifax, which arrived safely on 19 April 1943.

After two years of continuous service on the North Atlantic, *Napanee* was due for a major five-month refit, arriving in Montreal on 22 May 1943.[29] While in refit, her fo'c'sle was extended, her bridge rebuilt and improved, and two additional depth-charge throwers and 20-millimetre Oerlikon guns were installed.[30] Command of the ship was also passed to Acting Lieutenant Commander G.A. Powell, RCNVR. During an extended refit, the crew would be given leave and then a large number of the men would be transferred to other ships. As these men now had some experience, they were a valuable asset to the crews of the newly constructed ships.

The refit was completed by 21 October 1943 and *Napanee* worked up at Pictou, Nova Scotia, and returned to active service, still on the Newfie-Derry run with escort group C3.

On 6 December 1943, *Napanee* and her escort group were to be found leaving Pictou Harbour for another escort job. *Napanee* signalled the senior officer (SO), asking if he wanted *Napanee* to take the lead, and upon receiving an affirmative from the SO, made speed for the channel. HMCS *Milltown* was already in the channel, so *Napanee* increased speed

HMCS Napanee *as she appeared following an extensive refit in the summer of 1943. Her appearance had been changed significantly since she was built in 1941.*

CN-3522, Photo courtesy National Defence Imaging Library.

to overtake her and pass the ship on her starboard side. It is at this point that witnesses' and participants' recollections start to vary. *Napanee's* skipper stated that he kept a constant speed at 12.5 knots; *Milltown's* skipper also states he maintained his speed. But witnesses stated that as the two ships drew parallel to each other at a distance of only 50 yards, they saw each ship increasing speed as if they were racing. At this point the two ships created an area of suction between them, and, despite turning the rudder away, *Milltown* collided with *Napanee*. *Milltown* incurred the worst of the incident, with severe damage to her bows requiring four days to repair, and *Napanee* had a six-inch hole punched into her side near the deck line. The investigating

officer dismissed the reports of the two ships racing, stating in his report, "a Commanding Officer would never be inclined to risk their ship while engaging in a foolhardy race." Both commanding officers were cautioned to be more careful, and *Napanee's* skipper was admonished for failing to overtake a vessel in a safe manner.[31]

Over the next few months, work for *Napanee* was routine for the most part, with the exception of two minor incidents. In the first, she damaged some piles off the dock at the South Magazine Jetty in Bedford Basin when she was pushed away from the dock by the force of the tide; the ship was undamaged and the incident was considered to be a slight error in judgment.[32] The second occurred later in the new year, on 13 January

DND MC-2687A. Photo courtesy Archives and Collections Society, Picton.

HMCS Napanee, *outboard, in harbour with two sisters. HMCS* Orillia *is inboard and the centre corvette is unidentified.*

1944, when *Napanee* had to depart convoy HX 222 for a quick return to St. John's Harbour with an emergency appendix case and an asdic dome failure.[33] *Napanee* continued on the Newfie-Derry run until she left Londonderry for the last time and returned to Canada on 3 August 1944.

Napanee was again sent for refit, this time at Pictou, Nova Scotia, and then three weeks of work-ups in Bermuda. On return to Halifax she was assigned to escort group W2 on the "Triangle Run." The Triangle Run was escort duty on this side of the Atlantic Ocean, under the control of the Western Local Escort Force. The escort group would leave Halifax or Sydney, Nova Scotia, eastbound with a fast or slow convoy and escort it to the Mid-Ocean Meeting Point (MOMP) and hand it over to the Mid-Ocean

Escort Groups. They would then proceed to St. John's for fuel and afterwards escort another convoy heading westbound to New York City. Following a run ashore by the crews, the escort group would take a convoy from New York to Halifax to start the entire process again. *Napanee* remained with the W2 group until the end of the war.

On 15 January 1945, *Napanee* was involved in a minor collision with HMCS *Goderich*.[34] Although the damage to the two ships was minor, the incident itself could have been very serious, with the potential for loss of life and both ships. The day before, three merchant ships had been torpedoed in the approaches to Halifax Harbour, and every available escort was ordered out to search for the U-boat that had dared to prey on ships so close to Halifax.

Stern view of Napanee.

During the night, *Napanee* was performing an anti-submarine sweep in the Halifax approaches in a line-abreast formation with HMCS *Westmount* and HMCS *Penetang*. *Goderich* was ordered to close with one of the wrecked merchant ships and perform a search around the area at the same time,[35] as the German U-boat commanders would often use sunken wrecks to hide from the asdic. *Napanee* and *Goderich* approached each other in the darkness at the slow speed of eight knots. Both ships had radar, but it appears that neither officer-of-the-watch was paying attention to it. Just before the two ships collided, *Goderich* and *Napanee* spotted each other and made an emergency change of course to avoid the collision. Still, both ships collided, running side to side, but fortunately it was only a glancing blow.

The investigation that followed was very critical of both officers-of-the-watch and commanding officers. Perhaps most disturbing was that both commanding officers were in their cabins asleep at the time of the collision. The investigation found that under the circumstances, with their respective ships involved in an active submarine search in a confined channel with a large volume of traffic, their place was on the bridge. In a letter from Rear Admiral L.W. Murray, Commander-in-Chief, Canadian Northwest Atlantic, he writes, "That two ships should have come into collision when travelling at only eight knots shows very slow thinking, or inattention, on the part of the Officers-of-the-Watch concerned, though it is apparent that the action taken by GODERICH on seeing NAPANEE's port light

Photo courtesy Robert E.D. Hall.

HMCS Napanee *showing the Western Isles camouflage paint-scheme.*

at such short range, and by NAPANEE on becoming aware of GODERICH saved one or both ships from serious damage and probably serious loss of life." Murray also recommended a possible court martial for both officers-of-the-watch and commanding officers, but acknowledged that four trials would present more difficulties than the value to be gained.

Rear Admiral Murray summed up his letter, "It is recommended that the two Officers-of-the-Watch receive the severe displeasure of the Department. Captain (D) Halifax is being instructed to have the two Commanding Officers relieved of their commands as soon as suitable reliefs can be provided."[36]

Germany formally surrendered on 8 May 1945, ending the Battle of the Atlantic, though *Napanee* continued escorting convoys for the remainder of May to ensure that all U-boats had received the message and surrendered. She returned to Halifax from her last convoy on 31 May 1945.[37]

Napanee was paid off on 12 July 1945 at Sorel, Quebec. She was later purchased by Frankel Brothers of Toronto and was broken up at The Steel Company of Canada Limited in Hamilton, Ontario, in June 1946.

During the war, *Napanee* was well looked-after by the City of Napanee. The IODE,[38] Red Cross, and Napanee Collegiate and Vocational Institute were all sponsors of the ship. They provided the crew with ditty bags full of hand-knitted mitts, scarves, socks, balaclavas, and other assorted comforts including a piano. The girls from the school became pen pals to the crew, and the school provided a 16-millimetre Bell and Howell movie projector.

The city received many letters and Christmas cards thanking the citizens for their support of the ship, but very little information was received of the wartime activities, due to censorship. When *Napanee's* executive officer, Lieutenant Jim Stewart was decommissioned, he visited the city and presented the bell that was purchased by the city for the ship in 1940 to the town council. The side of the four-inch gun shield was also removed from the ship with the drawing of the Native head and submarine, also to be presented to the city in appreciation of the generous support for the ship and her crew. The bell and the-gun shield art were displayed in the council chambers for many years following the war. While the bell is now on display at the Lennox and Addington Museum in Napanee, the location of the gun shield is currently unknown, and the Historical Society is attempting to track it down.[39]

As a final note on HMCS *Napanee*, I would like to quote a newspaper article from Kingston concerning the launch of the ship. The article was published on 31 August 1940, and the final paragraph, wondering what the future would hold for this ship, actually foretold a gallant future for *Napanee* and her crew:

Photo courtesy Robert F.D. Hall.

8 August 1945, Lieutenant Jim Stewart, RCNR (right) at Dr. Hall's cottage, Bay of Quinte. Lieutenant Stewart accompanied by his mother and father had delivered the last White Ensign to fly on HMCS Napanee.

This particular ship may never have the opportunity of sending its name down in Canadian Naval History as the result of spectacular participation in an important naval battle, but it will, nonetheless, be engaged day in and day out in co-operation with other similar ships and with larger ships in doing a very useful and important job. And there is, of course, always the chance that the opportunity will arise for an historic bit of work under unusual circumstances. As the ship goes into the water, Kingston wishes her well.[40]

Photo courtesy Lennox and Addington County Museum, Napanee. Photographer Geoff Webster.

This bell was presented to HMCS Napanee by the town of Napanee and is now located at the Lennox and Addington County Museum.

AWARDS EARNED BY CREW

- Andrew Hedley Dobson, A/Lieutenant Commander, RCNR: Distinguished Service Cross (DSC)

   For distinguished services before the enemy.

- Duff Morrison Pennie, Warrant Engineer, RCN: Member, Order of the British Empire (MBE)

   This Officer has served continuously at sea since the outbreak of war in His Majesty's Canadian Destroyers and Corvettes. During this period, his outstanding skill, organizing ability and devotion to duty have resulted in a high standard of efficiency in his department. He has done much to improve the morale and spirit of the Service.

- James Wesley Vincent, Yeoman of Signals, RCNVR: Mention in Dispatches (MID)

   Throughout a total of thirty-two months service at sea during which period he was a survivor from HMCS Charlottetown, he has continually received excellent recommendations for good service and devotion to duty. His loyalty and zeal during his service in HMCS Napanee contributed in a high degree to the efficiency of this department and he has been a fine example to the Ship's Company as a whole.

Commanding Officers

A.H. Dobson, LCDR. RCNR	12 March 1941 to 8 December 1941
S. Henderson, LT. RCNR	9 December 1941 to 2 June 1944
G.A. Powell, A/LCDR, RCNVR	3 June 1944 to 12 July 1945

**HMCS *NAPANEE*
BATTLE HONOURS**

ATLANTIC   1941–1945

Specifications

Name:	HMCS *Napanee* for the City of Napanee, Ontario		
Classification:	Flower class, 1939–1940 program		
Builder:	Kingston Shipbuilding Company Limited — Kingston, Ontario		
Keel Laid: 20/03/40	Launched: 31/08/40	Commissioned: 12/05/41	Paid Off: 12/07/45
Length: 205 feet, 1 inch	Beam: 33 feet, 1 inch	Draught: 11 feet	
Displacement: 950 tons	Speed: 16 knots	Endurance: 3,450 nautical miles at 12 knots	Fuel: 230 tons
Crew: 2 officers, 48 other ranks (later 6 officers, 79 other ranks)	Machinery: 4 cycle triple expansion engine, two Scotch marine boilers		
Armament (as built):	- one 4 inch BL Mk. IX gun — forward gun platform - two twin 0.5 inch machine guns — after gun tub - two single .303 inch machine guns — bridge wings - two depth charge throwers — waist - two depth charge rails — stern - 40 depth charges - minesweeping gear		
Post-refit (October 1943):	- one 4 inch BL Mk. IX gun — forward gun platform - one 2-pdr. pom-pom Mk VIII gun — after gun tub - two single 20mm Oerlikon machine guns — bridge wings - four depth charge throwers — waist - two depth charge rails — stern - 70 depth charges		

Specifications of HMCS Napanee *as built and post-refit.*

Chart prepared by Roger Litwiller.

CHAPTER 3

HMCS *BELLEVILLE*
K332
REVISED FLOWER-CLASS
CORVETTE
INCREASED ENDURANCE
1943–1944 PROGRAM

A-1023-R. Photo courtesy National Defence Imaging Library.

HMCS Belleville *newly commissioned on 23 October 1944.*

BUILT AT KINGSTON SHIPYARDS AS HULL number 29,[1] HMCS *Belleville* belonged to one of the last groups of corvettes to be ordered before the end of the Second World War. She was christened *Belleville* on 6 June 1944 at her launching ceremony, by Mrs. Harry Rollins, the wife of Belleville mayor Harry Rollins. The ship remained at Kingston fitting out and was commissioned into the Royal Canadian Navy on the 19 October 1944. Her first commanding officer was Lieutenant J.E. Korning, RCNVR, already a veteran of the Battle of Atlantic at the age of 26.[2]

On 22 October 1944, there was an official adoption ceremony of HMCS *Belleville* by the city of Belleville. From ten o'clock in the morning until three o'clock in the afternoon, over 2,000 people toured the corvette berthed at the Canada Steamship Lines dock in Kingston. To receive the visitors, the ship was dressed in her signal flags from stem to stern, while the Royal Canadian Naval Band from St. Hyacinthe played stirring nautical tunes.

At precisely three o'clock, the ship's bell was rung six times and the decks were cleared of all visitors

HMCS Belleville *under construction at the Kingston Shipbuilding Yards.*

Belleville *was the second last corvette to be launched at Kingston.*

Excellent photograph of Belleville's *triple-expansion engine being lowered into the ship.*

except the ceremonial party located on the bridge. The adoption ceremony began. Honoured guests included Mayor Harry Rollins; Captain (N) G.L. Roome, supervisor of contract-built ships; Mr. J.B. Boyce, chairman of the Belleville Corvette Committee; Mr. G.H. Stokes, member of Parliament; Lieutenant-Colonels B.C. Sisler and B.C. Donnan; Mr. O. Duff, Canadian National Railways; as well as numerous council members from Belleville and Hastings County.

Many speeches were given expressing how the ship would benefit from the variety of gifts supplied by the community and her citizens. In his speech, Captain (N) G.L. Roome said, "the people of Belleville should be proud of this corvette. It was with greatest regret that we discovered it was impossible to bring the ship to its parent city. Please thank the residents of Belleville, the Navy appreciates what they have done for this ship."[3]

Photo courtesy RCSCC Quinte.

HMCS Belleville *during adoption ceremony in Kingston. The curator of the Naval Museum of the Great Lakes in Kingston identifies the building as the Canada Steamship Lines building.*

Photo courtesy RCSCC Quinte.

A member of Belleville*'s crew shows a guest the ropes during a tour.*

Belleville left Kingston for the first time on 24 October 1944 and travelled to Toronto, Ontario, for gun trials, docking at pier 6 at the foot of York Street the same day.[4] She returned to Kingston the following day, and then departed the Great Lakes on 28 October en route to Montreal, arriving on 29 October.

She remained in Montreal until 11 November 1944, when she departed for Halifax in company with her identical sister ships *Lachute* and *West York*.

Belleville reported that she still had many defects and incomplete components when she sailed, including problems with her hull, machinery, electrical systems, and gunnery and anti-submarine equipment. All three ships arrived in Halifax on 13 November.[5]

Upon arrival at Halifax, she continued fitting out and repairing defects until 17 January 1945, when she sailed for Bermuda for training and workups. She was joined by HMCS *Fredericton*, also a corvette, who was just out of refit after four years of service on the North Atlantic. On the way south, the two corvettes were to pick up two oil tankers, SS *Esso Paterson* and SS *Great Meadows*, at the Halifax Gate and escort them to a point west of Boston. From there the tankers were to proceed independently to their destinations. The two corvettes arrived in Bermuda on 20 January.[6]

Belleville remained in Bermuda for one month, completing her evolutions, and departed back to Halifax on 20 February 1945. While en route north, she was diverted to assist in escorting convoy BX 146, sailing from Boston to Halifax and consisting of 24 merchant ships.[7] On 23 January, *Belleville* was

Photo courtesy Roger Litwiller.

Name Plate for HMCS Belleville, *donated by the City of Belleville, now displayed at City Hall.*

A-1025-R. Photo courtesy National Defence Imaging Library.

"HMCS Belleville *newly commissioned into the RCN, pays a visit to the City of Belleville on 23 October 1944." Newspaper reports from the time have Captain G.L. Roome, supervisor of contract-built shipping, apologizing for not being able to have the ship visit the city, citing that the Bay of Quinte was not deep enough for a corvette to enter.*

"Beneath the Barber Pole"

Surgeon-Lieutenant W.A. Paldon

Tune: Road to the Isles

1. It's away! Outward the swinging fo'c'sles reel
From the smoking seas' white glare upon the stand —
It's the gray miles that are slipping under keel
When we're rolling outward-bound from Newfoundland!

6. From Halifax or Newfiejohn or Derry's clustered towers
By trackless paths where conning towers roll
If you know another group in which you'd sooner spend your hours
You've never sailed beneath the Barber Pole!

Chart created by Roger Litwiller.

Two verses of the song "Beneath the Barber Pole."

detached from her first convoy due to engine defects and returned to Halifax with HMCS *Noranda*, who was escorting four stragglers from the convoy.[8] It would take several weeks to repair her engines.

On 8 March 1945, *Belleville* received minor damage to her stern while being moved by tugs.[9] Following repairs, on 26 March she was assigned to active duty with escort group C5, the famous "Barber Pole Squadron" based at St. John's, Newfoundland, escorting convoys to Londonderry and Northern Ireland. The other ships of the squadron included the frigates HMCS *Runnymede*, HMCS *St. Stephen*, and corvettes HMCS *Lachute* and HMCS *West York*. The squadron was called "Barber Pole" because the funnel tops of its ships were painted with red and white stripes, similar to a barber's pole, to identify them. In 1943 the Barber Pole Squadron had a song written about them called "Beneath the Barber Pole."

HMCS *Belleville* arrived at St. John's on 27 March 1945. She was to leave with escort group C5 to escort convoy HX 346 the next day, but her departure was delayed again due to defects, and she joined the convoy later.[10] The convoy had departed from New York City four days earlier, bound for Liverpool with 61 ships.

On the way across, *Belleville* lost her asdic and later her radar broke down, leaving the ship with only the naked eye augmented by binoculars for searching and detecting the enemy.[11] The ocean crossing was uneventful until the convoy approached Holyhead, Wales, on 7 April. Unknown to the escorts, *U-1024* was lying in wait. The German submarine had been on the bottom when she heard the convoy approaching, and her skipper was able to place his submarine between the escorts and the merchant ships of the convoy. He was in such an excellent attack position that he had to crash dive for fear of being accidentally run over by the first ship in the port column.

Once the danger had passed, the submarine returned to periscope depth and fired one torpedo at the unsuspecting convoy. The target was SS *James W. Nesmith*, the fourth ship in the port column. She was hit in the port quarter and slowed to a stop; fortunately for her and her crew the ship did not sink, although the damage was severe.

The escorts of the convoy raced to find the German submarine, assuming the attack had come from ahead and not from within the convoy itself. In fact, *U-1024* had continued down the convoy and past the rear of the column to make her escape. The only escort in her path was *Belleville*.

Unfortunately, *Belleville's* asdic and radar were still not in service and the submarine escaped directly under her, undetected.

Belleville's lookouts were determined, however, and when the sun set they spotted what appeared to be a periscope on the surface. She made a run in and dropped a pattern of depth charges, with no effect. Twice more the periscope was spotted by the lookouts and two more attacks were made. It was then that they realized what they believed to be a periscope was indeed a seabird called a Dipchick. This is a large seabird, similar to our loons, and when on the water with only its head and neck appear above the surface, appearing similar to a periscope in the failing light of dusk.

DND MC-2107. Photo courtesy Archive and Collection Society, Picton.

Picture of Belleville *looking aft from the bridge. The barber pole markings are clearly visible on her funnel, with the maple leaf below.*

Belleville took the crippled freighter in tow and left the convoy, escorted by HMCS *Huntsville*. A corvette was not designed to tow a ship the size of the SS *James W. Nesmith*, a Liberty ship, and as they started to tow her the cable separated and broke. A second attempt was made and some progress achieved, until the tow cable broke a second time. At this point *Belleville* went alongside the freighter to secure and tow/push the freighter the 12 miles to port. When *Belleville*'s skipper called up to the ship to pass down their berthing lines, they received no answer from the crew. Finally, the freighter's master leaned over the side, quite drunk along with the rest of his crew. They had decided since

they had nothing more to do they would celebrate their good fortune of not being sunk. Only when Lieutenant Korning threatened to put an armed party aboard the freighter did the crew co-operate and pass the berthing lines down to *Belleville*.

The tow was slow and arduous for *Belleville*, with several lines breaking and snapping at the tow's end. One of her officers was flipped on his back as one of the lines snapped and caught his ankle. They finally made the breakwater of the port and with one final push the ship was now safely in harbour, but again the lines separated. This time the freighter's crew refused to assist *Belleville*, and she was forced to send over

DND MC-2102, Photo courtesy Archive and Collection Society, Picton.

Bow photo of Belleville *showing the False Hull camouflage scheme.*

a boarding party. *Belleville*'s crew then brought the freighter to a shoal and dropped her anchor, when it became apparent just how serious the damage to the freighter was: as *Belleville* cleared the ship, it sank on the shoal, coming to rest on the shallow bottom.[12]

James W. Nesmith had been carrying a load of tobacco and aircraft. Following the war, Lieutenant Korning placed a salvage claim for the freighter, acting as agent for the officers and crew of HMCS *Belleville*. When a ship is salvaged, the rescue crew is entitled to compensation based on the value of the ship and its cargo. Due to the fact that ships from so many countries were actively salvaging and being salvaged, the nightmare of settling accounts was resolved by simply agreeing that most salvage claims were to be considered paid in full, without money ever changing hands. There is no record of *Belleville*'s crew receiving any compensation for their efforts.

U-1024 carried on for the next four days following the attack on *James W. Nesmith*, when finally she was located and attacked, incurring some minor damage, but again slipped her attackers. Then she made an attack on convoy BB80 on 12 April 1945 and hit the freighter SS *Will Rogers*. This time the escorts found their target and attacked without mercy. *U-1024* was forced to the surface when her machinery was damaged by the depth charges, and her crew abandoned the submarine. Thirty-seven of the submarine's crew were rescued and became prisoners of war.

Belleville and her escort group departed Londonderry on 16 April 1945 with convoy ON 297, consisting of 81 ships bound for New York City. The escort group was relieved by the Western Local Escort Group and returned to St. John's, on 29 April.[13]

Starboard-side view of Belleville. *Her whaler has been lowered and the crew has gathered in the waist and stern of the ship.*

On 7 May 1945, the day before Germany surrendered, Lieutenant Commander R.M. Powell, RCNVR, took over command as *Belleville*'s second and final commanding officer.

She sailed with her last convoy on 13 May 1945. Convoy HX 355 had departed New York City on 9 May en route to Liverpool with 57 ships, because although the war was officially over, no one could be certain if all the U-boats had received the order to surrender and some could still be stalking the merchant ships. The convoy arrived in Londonderry on 25 May without incident.[14]

Four days later, *Belleville*, along with HMCS *Hallowell*, HMCS *Giffard*, and HMCS *Arnprior*, departed from the United Kingdom for the last time. *Belleville* had with her 25 passengers returning to St. John's. This trip with *Hallowell* marks the only time the two Bay of Quinte ships worked together. All four ships arrived in St. John's, on 4 June.[15]

On 8 June 1945, *Belleville* departed St. John's for Halifax to begin de-storing and prepare for paying off. She was paid off at Sorel, Quebec, on 5 July 1945.

She remained at Sorel, until she was sold in 1947 to the Dominican Navy and was renamed *Juan Bautista Cambiaso*.[16] She remained in service with their navy until she was broken up in 1972.

Photo courtesy Roger Litwiller

The bell from HMCS Belleville *is at the Royal Canadian Sea Cadet Corps Quinte in Belleville, Ontario.*

Commanding Officers

J.E. Korning, LT, RCN	19 October 1944 to 6 March 1945
R.M. Powell, LCDR, RCNVR	7 March 1945 to 5 July 1945

**HMCS *BELLEVILLE*
BATTLE HONOURS**

ATLANTIC   **1945**

Specifications

Name:	HMCS *Belleville*, for the City of Belleville
Classification:	Revised Flower class, increased endurance, 1943–1944 program
Builder:	Kingston Shipbuilding Company Limited — Kingston, Ontario

Keel Laid:	Launched:	Commissioned:	Paid Off:
21/01/44	17/06/44	19/09/44	05/07/45

Length:	Beam:	Draught:	
209 feet, 4 inches	33 feet, 1 inch	11 feet	

Displacement:	Speed:	Endurance: 7,400	Fuel:
970 tons	16 knots	nautical miles at 10 knots	338 tons

Crew: 7 officers, 90 other ranks	Machinery: 4 cycle triple expansion engine, two water tube boilers

Armament:	- one 4 inch QF Mk. XIX gun — forward gun platform
	- one twin 20mm Oerlikon machine gun — after gun tub
	- two single 2mm Oerlikon machine guns — bridge wings
	- one Hedgehog anti-submarine mortar — forward gun platform
	- four depth charge throwers — waist
	- depth charge rails — stern
	- 100 depth charges

Specifications of HMCS Belleville.

Chart prepared by Roger Litwiller.

CHAPTER 4

HMCS *Hallowell*
K666
River Class
Frigate
1943–1944 Program

CN-3499, Photo courtesy National Defence Imaging Library

HMCS Hallowell *at Victoria Pier, Montreal, after commissioning on 8 August 1944.*

THE PROPOSED NAME FOR THIS SHIP was initially *Picton*, for Picton, Ontario, in Prince Edward County. *Picton* was rejected as a name because the RCN already had a ship by the name of HMCS *Pictou* and the two names sounded too similar. Athol, a nearby township, was also suggested and for the same reason rejected, as an HMCS *Atholl* was already active. Glenora for the community south of Picton was rejected because several Royal Navy ships had similar names, as well as one of our own Glen-class tugs, some of which were constructed in Trenton by Central Bridge.

Hallowell from Hallowell Township was then suggested as the name for the ship, as the township originally included Picton, Athol Township, and both South and North Marysburg Townships. The name originated from one of the early landowners in the area: Benjamin Hallowell, a Loyalist from Boston, who was given a 1,000-acre parcel of land in Prince Edward County and resided in Toronto. His son, Benjamin Hallowell Junior, left Canada for England and joined the Royal Navy. He fought under Lord Nelson as captain of HMS *Swiftsure* at the Battle of the Nile and was Mentioned in Dispatches by Nelson at the time. Captain Hallowell sailed his 74-gun ship close to the pride of the French Navy, *L'Orient*, with its 120 guns, and outshot the superior French ship at point-blank range. To celebrate his victory he sent his friend, Lord Admiral Nelson, a coffin as a gift. Accompanying the coffin was a note, wishing Nelson a long life and noting that when the time came he could be buried in a prize of battle, for the coffin was made from the mainmast of *L'Orient*. The gift pleased Nelson very much and he kept the coffin behind his chair in HMS *Vanguard*. When the sad day came at the Battle of Trafalgar and Nelson was killed as his fleet claimed victory over the French, Hallowell's gift was to meet its intended usage.[1] When Benjamin Hallowell married into a wealthy English family, he added Carew to his name. Later, he was knighted and became Vice Admiral Sir Benjamin Hallowell Carew.[2] The ship name *Hallowell* was accepted and received royal approval, and the communities of Prince Edward County readily stood behind their ship.

H.M.C.S. "HALLOWELL"

Built and Engined by
CANADIAN VICKERS LIMITED
MONTREAL, CANADA

Keel laid November 5, 1943 • Launched March 28, 1944 • Completed in July 1944

Hallowell – Prince Edward County – Province of Ontario – Canada, was visited for the first time by the loyalists in 1784 – founded in 1797. The name "Hallowell" was given in honour of Benjamin Hallowell, who was a prominent loyalist, and formerly from Boston. The first meeting of the municipality took place in 1798. Amongst the first pioneers were Major Peter Vanalstine and Lieutenant Paul Huff. The first house was inhabited by Colonel Archibald MacDonald and was built by shipbuilders. ⁅ Picton, founded in 1830, is an important town in Hallowell Township. A Canal was constructed between Picton and Prescott the same year. In 1830, the "Hallowell Free Press" was put into operation. ⁅ Benjamin Hallowell was knighted and subsequently became an Admiral in the Royal Navy. The name Carew was added to his own after his marriage to Mrs. Carew. Sir Benjamin fought as a Captain under Viscount Lord Nelson at the battle of the Nile. In the biographical memoirs of Nelson, published in 1806, it is recorded that Captain (later Admiral) Hallowell had been mentioned in despatches by Nelson. ⁅ It may be said, therefore, that H.M.C.S. "Hallowell" has been named after one of Lord Nelson's Captains. ⁅ Shown below is an authentic impression of the signature of Vice-Admiral Sir Benjamin Hallowell Carew, taken from the Carlton House Register in London, England, and dated September 11th, 1828.

The signature of Sir Benj. Hallowell Carew and certain of the above information was obtained through the courtesy of Mr. C. G. Hallowell of Paris, Ontario, a distant relative of Sir Benjamin.

Certificate presented to the citizens of Prince Edward County by Canadian Vickers Ltd.

Crew photo of HMCS Hallowell *on the day of her commissioning.*

HMCS *Hallowell* was constructed at Canadian Vickers Limited in Montreal, Quebec, at a cost of $1,400,000. Prior to *Hallowell*'s launch, the river in the area had to be blasted to clear the ice,[3] and she was released with great ceremony into the still-frozen water of the St. Lawrence River on 28 March 1944. Her sponsor was Mrs. John Poole, wife of one of the oldest employees at the company. Several dignitaries from the area travelled to Montreal for the launching, including the mayor of Picton, Nesbitt McKibbon,

and his wife; Fred Ward, Picton Township Clerk; R.S. McQuade and Clarence Mallory, Reeve and clerk for Hallowell Township; and George G. Justin, local member of Parliament.

The launch day established two Canadian shipbuilding records: *Hallowell* was the first ship to be launched on the St. Lawrence River that year, but also the earliest a ship had been launched from the Vickers ways. A third record was matched when HMCS *Stone Town* was launched one hour later from

R.C.N. Photo courtesy of the Archives and Collections Society, Picton.

Equipment being transferred to HMCS Hallowell *by jackstay while at sea.*

the same yard, meeting the Canadian record for two naval ships launched in the same day.[4] Also, three 10,000-ton park ships were launched at the nearby United Shipyards, bringing the total to five ships launched in Montreal in one day.[5]

A week before *Hallowell* was completed, a ceremony was held in her as one of her officers, Lieutenant Alfred W. Best, a native of Toronto, was decorated with the George Medal by Captain J.E.W. Oland, naval officer in charge at Montreal. Lieutenant Best was awarded the decoration for his part in an earlier action, when he led a boarding party onto a burning oil tanker and saved the vessel.[6]

On 8 August 1944 she was commissioned, under command of Skipper Lieutenant E.S.P. Pleasance, RCNR. A delegation of Prince Edward County citizens attended the ceremony and contributed to the comforts of her crew, offering, amongst other contributions, two washing machines to be installed and also, the heart of a ship, her bell.[7] She left for Halifax and arrived there on 3 September.

Hallowell departed for training evolutions and workups in Bermuda on 30 September 1944 with HMCS *Kapuskasing*. While in Bermuda, she ran into difficulty from the moment she arrived. As the two ships were docking, *Hallowell*'s bow collided with *Kapuskasing*, slicing three feet into her hull and causing serious flooding. This required *Kapuskasing* to be sent to dry dock for survey and repairs. *Hallowell* was more fortunate: she had her bow bent and about 40 rivets loose. The investigation found that the engine room telegraphs were located in such a way that the artificer could not clearly see both of them from any one position in the room. Consequently, one engine was left in the ahead position when the bridge had called for "All Stop."[8] The inquiry found Lieutenant Pleasance to blame, but added that "no disciplinary action was to be taken." The report went on to caution the engineering officer to implement better supervision in the engine room.[9]

Unfortunately, a few days later, on 17 October 1944, *Hallowell* was again involved in a collision, this time with a U.S. Army scow while she was trying to secure to a buoy. The collision occurred 41 minutes after her first attempt to secure herself to the buoy, and then it still took over an hour to finally secure the ship. The commanding officer of the training establishment, HMCS *Somers Isle*, recommended, "It is considered that the blame is entirely attributable to the Commanding Officer who is consistently found in trouble in handling his ship. No disciplinary action is proposed other than the removal of the Commanding Officer." Command of *Hallowell* was given to Lieutenant Commander R.H. Angus, RCNVR on 19 October 1944.[10]

The damage to *Hallowell* was confined to a bent stem, loose rivets, and six small fractures to her bow plating, all of which was repaired in Bermuda at a cost of 30 pounds.[11] She returned to Halifax in early November and was assigned to escort group C1.

She left from St. John's on 28 November with her first convoy, HX 322 The convoy departed New York City on 24 November with 38 ships, had an uneventful crossing, and arrived at Liverpool on 8 December.

From December onward, *Hallowell* was designated senior officer of escort group C1, and she remained with C1 until the end of the war. She operated continuously as mid-ocean escort until June 1945, crossing the Atlantic Ocean a total of nine times.

RCN. Photo courtesy of the Archives and Collections Society, Picton.

HMCS Hallowell, *possibly in Bermuda, in October 1944; her crew is enjoying a "SwimEx" off the port side.*

Photo courtesy Naval Museum of Manitoba.

CN-3291. Photo courtesy National Defence Imaging Library.

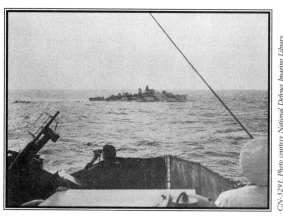

HMCS Hallowell *in a moderate sea. Her pristine paint is almost gone.*

HMCS Hallowell.

Photo courtesy Naval Museum of Manitoba.

Excellent picture of Hallowell*'s bow and bridge. Her hedgehog is clearly visible on the fo'c'scle.*

During one of these crossings, in January 1945, *Hallowell* and her escort group left the United Kingdom with a convoy bound for Canadian and United States ports. The convoy was battered by a succession of severe North Atlantic winter storms; repeatedly, the convoy would be buffeted by high winds and seas and the ships would be scattered. The escorts would then slowly return the ships to the convoy, only to be scattered again and again over successive days. At one point the wind-speed indicator located on a MAC ship[12] assigned to the convoy read speeds of 80 to 90 knots, or over 100 miles per hour. This forced the convoy to heave-to and wait out the storm. Finally, after 23 days at sea, the escort was relieved by the Western Escort Force and put into St. John's Harbour.[13]

The war in Europe ended on 8 May 1945, and *Hallowell* departed Greenock, Scotland, for the last time early on 29 May with 18 passengers returning to St. John's. She was in company with *Belleville*, *Arnprior*, and *Giffard*. All four ships crossed the Atlantic Ocean with their navigation lights blazing for the first time — convoy and blackout restrictions had been lifted at midnight on the 28th.

On 3 June the ships encountered thick fog and icebergs off the Grand Banks. *Hallowell*, *Belleville*, *Arnprior*, and *Giffard* arrived in St. John's on 4 June.[14] This is the only time two of the Bay of Quinte ships worked together.

During the months of July and August, *Hallowell* was engaged in operations on Canada's East Coast. She departed St. John's on 11 June with passengers travelling

Very rare aerial picture of HMCS Hallowell.

R.C.N. Photo courtesy of the Archives and Collections Society, Picton.

to for Quebec City, arriving there on 14 June. After a short stay, she returned to St. John's on the 18th.

Hallowell's next escort duty also marked her first contact with an enemy submarine. She departed St. John's on 21 June with passengers for Halifax, but also in her charge was the surrendered German submarine *U-190*.[15] *U-190* had formally surrendered to HMCS *Victoriaville* and HMCS *Thorlock* on 11 May. Three simple lines on Department of National Defence letterhead secured the submarine's fate: "I hereby unconditionally surrender German Submarine *U-190* to the Royal Canadian Navy through the Flag Officer, Newfoundland." *U-190* was the submarine that torpedoed and sank HMCS *Esquimalt* on 16 April 1945, five miles off Chebucto Head, near Halifax. Thirty-nine of *Esquimalt's* crew lost their lives in the attack.

Hallowell returned to St. John's on 26 June and was engaged in exercises for three days, commencing on 3 July 1945. She made another trip to Halifax on 8 July with passengers and returned to St. John's later in the month on the 24th. On 5 August 1945, she received her third and final commanding officer, Lieutenant D. Davis, RCNVR.

Many of the Canadian frigates were selected for a tropicalization refit so they could continue to fight the war in the Pacific. *Hallowell* was one of the ships selected for this refit, but with the sudden end to the war, with Japan's unconditional surrender, the refit was cancelled.[16]

HMCS *Hallowell* was paid off on 7 November 1945 at Shelburne and placed in reserve for disposal. Unlike a large number of her sister frigates, *Hallowell* was not selected for modernization and conversion to a Prestonian-class ocean escort, to enjoy an extended life with the RCN.

RCN, Photo courtesy of the Archives and Collections Society, Picton.

HMCS Hallowell *approaching the stern of an unknown corvette.*

Hallowell was sold in 1946 to Uruguayan interests and converted to merchant service. Later, in 1949, she was resold to a Palestinian firm and converted to a short-service Mediterranean ferry and renamed *Sharon*.

In 1952 she was acquired by the Israeli Navy, restored as a warship, and renamed *Misgave* (K-30). She was re-armed with three 120 millimetre Italian guns, two 40 millimetre guns, and eight 20 millimetre guns. She was one of the primary ships in the fledgling Israeli Navy along with two other retired Canadian warships, HMCS *Stathadam* and HMCS *Violetta*, becoming *Mitvah* (K-28) and *Miznak* (K-32) respectively.

In July of 1953, all three ships provided assistance to the earthquake victims in the islands of Zante and

Photo courtesy of the Archives and Collections Society, Picton.

Hallowell's bell was presented to the Town of Picton on 19 February 1947.

Kefalonia in Greece. During the Israeli Sinai Campaign in October 1956, she patrolled the southern shores of Israel and participated in shelling the Gaza Strip and Rafiah.[17] She remained with the Israeli Navy until she was sold for the last time, in 1959, to the Sinhalese (Sri Lanka) Navy and renamed *Gajabahu*.

In 1978 *Hallowell* was finally discarded, after having the single longest career of all the Bay of Quinte ships. She had gone from warship to merchant ship, then to ferry and back to warship. She served with distinction in three navies and in the waters of North America, Europe, the Mediterranean, and the Indian Ocean.

AWARDS EARNED BY CREW

- George Stanley Hall, Acting Commander, RCNR: Mention in Dispatches (MID)

  This Officer has served almost continuously at sea for four years in command of H.M.C. Ships. His long and varied experience in the Merchant Service in peace time has assisted him to become a most valuable and efficient Senior Officer. His unswerving loyalty and strict sense of duty are in accordance with the highest traditions of the Royal Canadian Navy.

- Earnest S. N. Pleasance, Skipper Lieutenant, RCNR: Mention in Dispatches (MID)

   This officer has served at sea for over three years in His Majesty's Canadian Ships engaged in minesweeping and escort work, lately in command. During the whole of that time he has shown himself to be most trustworthy and hard working, and has set an excellent example to others by his devotion to duty.

- Donald Davis, Lieutenant, RCNVR: Mention in Dispatches (MID)

   For services in the invasion of Normandy.

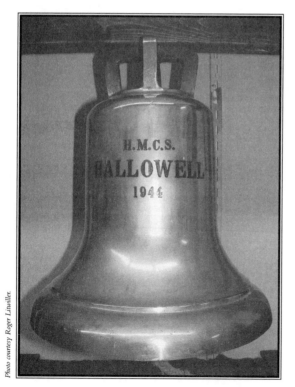

Photo courtesy Roger Litwiller.

HMCS Hallowell's bell is on display at the Mariners Park Museum in Prince Edward County, Ontario.

Commanding Officers

E.S.N. Pleasance, SKPR/LT, RCNR	8 August 1944 to 18 October 1944
R.H. Angus, LCDR, RCNVR	19 October 1944 to 4 August 1945
D. Davis, LT, RCNVR	5 August 1945 to 7 November 1945

HMCS *HALLOWELL*
BATTLE HONOURS

ATLANTIC   1944–1945

Specifications

Name:	HMCS *Hallowell*, alternate name for Picton		
Classification:	River-class frigate, 1943–1944 program		
Builder:	Canadian Vickers Limited — Montreal, Quebec		
Keel Laid: 22/11/43	Launched: 28/03/44	Commissioned: 08/08/44	Paid Off: 07/11/45
Length: 301 feet, 6 inches	Beam: 36 feet, 7 inches	Draught: 9 feet	
Displacement: 1,445 tons	Speed: 19 knots	Endurance: 7,200 nautical miles at 12 knots	Fuel: 440 tons
Crew: 8 officers, 133 other ranks	Machinery: two admiralty 3 drum boilers, two shafts, reciprocating triple expansion engine		
Armament:	- two 4 inch QF Mk. XIX guns — forward gun platform - one 12-pdr. pom-pom gun — after gun platform - eight 20mm Oerlikon twin mounted machine guns — 2 bridge wings/2 waist - one Hedgehog anti submarine mortar — fo'c'sle - four depth charge throwers — waist - depth charge rails — stern - 145 depth charges		

Chart prepared by Roger Litwiller.

Specifications of HMCS Quinte.

CHAPTER 5

HMCS *QUINTE*
J166
BANGOR CLASS
MINESWEEPER
1939–1940 PROGRAM

HMCS Quinte *J166, Bangor-class minesweeper. 1939–1940 Program.*

HMCS *QUINTE* WAS NAMED AFTER the Bay of Quinte, which is itself believed to be a corruption of the name given by the Iroquois to an old village situated near Rice Lake. The French geographers extended the name to include an area east of the village to what is now the Bay of Quinte, off Lake Ontario.[1]

The ship was built at the Burrard Dry Dock Company Limited in Vancouver, British Columbia, and she is the only Bay of Quinte ship to be constructed on the west coast of Canada. Her keel was laid down on 14 December 1940, and she was commissioned into the Royal Canadian Navy on 30 August 1941, under the command of Lieutenant C.A. Nicol, RCNR. *Quinte* was built at a cost of $669,600.[2]

Her departure from Esquimalt, British Columbia, was delayed by one day due to poor weather, and she left on 10 October en route to Halifax with HMCS *Clayoquot* and HMCS *Ungava*. The small fleet made fuelling and rest stops at San Pedro and Manzanillo, Mexico, arriving at Balboa, the Pacific entrance to the Panama Canal, on 29 October 1941. The ships passed through the canal, leaving the Atlantic side the next day, and sailed north to Kingston, Jamaica, arriving there on 1 November.[3]

Photo courtesy Canada Department of National Defence/Library and Archives Canada/PA-128265.

HMCS Quinte, *Esquimalt, B.C., 3 September 1941.*

Although *Quinte* was a minesweeper, she was seldom employed as such, and most of her work would be escorting convoys. Her first job involved neither minesweeping nor convoy escort duties, but rather those of a tugboat. While in Jamaica, on 3 November 1941, she was diverted to assist the Royal Navy aircraft carrier HMS *Indomitable,* which was aground at Kingston, Jamaica. There were no locally available tugs capable of pulling the 23,000-ton aircraft carrier free. *Quinte,* together with her sister HMCS *Clayoquot* and the Royal Navy corvette HMS *Clarkia,* got to

work and pulled the big ship free. During the process, *Clarkia* also grounded and the two minesweepers had to pull her free.[4] The two minesweepers and the corvette combined weighed not quite 10 percent of the aircraft carrier's total weight.

The towing operation delayed *Quinte*'s departure from Jamaica by one day, and she left on 5 November to Bermuda. Arriving there on 10 November, after one day in port, she proceeded to Halifax. *Quinte, Clayoquot,*[5] and *Ungava* arrived in Halifax on 14 November 1941. The passage from the Pacific Ocean to the Atlantic Ocean took a total of 35 days.[6]

Quinte was given time for repairs and the training of her crew. She was first assigned to Western Local Escort Force (WLEF) under general escort duties, escorting convoys on our East Coast between ports in Nova Scotia, New Brunswick, Newfoundland, and Boston. Sometimes she would escort the convoys to a meeting point at sea and sometimes to a mid-ocean point off St. John's.

Her first convoy was HX 170; this was a small convoy of 29 ships departing from Halifax on 13 January 1942, proceeding to Liverpool. *Quinte* escorted the convoy on the first leg of the route until relieved by the Mid-Ocean Escort Group.

Quinte and her crew then spent the next five months escorting a total of 25 convoys on this side of the Atlantic.[7] On 20 May 1942, *Quinte* was transferred to Halifax Force for convoy escort.[8]

On 24 May 1942, Quinte went to the aid of the freighter SS *Anna Mazaraki* of Greece, aground on Cape Sable. She stood by the stricken ship until relieved by HMCS *Weyburn*, who was escorting the salvage tug *Security*. Unfortunately, as with most ships that find the shoals off Cape Sable, she could not be recovered and became a total loss.[9]

At the end of July 1942, *Quinte* was sent to reinforce convoy ON 113, which had left Liverpool on 13 July with 35 merchant ships. While crossing the Atlantic Ocean, the convoy was attacked by several U-boats, and three merchant ships were sunk and one damaged. She joined the convoy at the end of the battle and there were no further attacks.[10]

Later, on 4 September 1942, *Quinte* was ordered to escort the salvage tug *Foundation Franklin* to the assistance of a ship on fire due east of Cape Cod.[11]

The unspecified vessel was en route to New York City when she had apparently caught fire. When *Quinte* arrived on scene, she found the U.S. fleet auxiliary ship USS *Wakefield* was the ship to be rescued, but she was not alone. In her company were three U.S. destroyers, six U.S. tugs, and one U.S. minesweeper — no one had reported the presence of an operational U.S. salvage force.[12]

Quinte was later given an extensive refit at Lunenburg, Nova Scotia, commencing on 14 October 1942. The ship was well in need of a refit: she had been continually employed, save for a few days here and there to repair defects in the ship, since departing Esquimalt on 30 October 1941. During the course of the refit, extensive alterations were made to her bridge structure, electronics, and compasses.

On 22 November 1942, the commanding officer of *Quinte* was handed a message: "On completion of trials at Lunenburg, being in all respects ready for sea, proceed to take fuel from HMCS *Ungava* and proceed to Pictou, N.S. departing Lunenburg on 27 November 1942."[13]

Quinte's refit was completed on 26 November 1942. Her sister ship, *Ungava*, was also in Lunenburg for a refit and was not yet finished, so *Quinte* was to take fuel from her. Unfortunately, *Ungava* was not sent the same message, and consequently her commanding officer refused *Quinte* any additional fuel. The estimate was that *Quinte* had 52 tons of fuel aboard and that was more than enough for the trip to Pictou, the distance being only 272 miles or about 27 hours steaming time.[14]

Because the sailing orders were to have *Quinte* depart Lunenburg the day after the refit was complete, there was only time for a cursory check of her systems, and all appeared to be in working order.

Port-side view of HMCS Quinte.

At 1830 *Quinte*'s commanding officer, Lieutenant C.A. Nicol, took his ship to sea. Fifteen minutes later, he had the minesweeping gear lowered on the starboard side to sweep the channel out of Lunenburg Harbour. When the ship was five miles outside the Lunenburg buoy, the minesweeping gear was recovered and a fix was taken to determine the termination of the sweep. This was when the navigating officer realized the gyro compass repeater on the bridge was seriously defective. Up to this point, the ship's course had been accurate, and so she continued on her way despite the faulty equipment and made the Sambro light vessel on time at 2300, passing at a distance of one mile. Thirty minutes later, *Quinte* altered course to the north. At 0145 a good fix of their position was made off Egg Island, placing *Quinte* in the correct position and course.[15]

During the course of the night, the wind and sea became increasingly violent, pounding the ship and knocking its speed down to 10 knots. As daylight came on 28 November, the crew found that the storm had caused some damage and the radio aerials had been carried away. They could no longer transmit or receive radio messages, but as they were under radio silence most of the time, it did not affect their transit to Pictou.

At 1045 the navigating officer was on watch and discovered the gyro steering compass had a severe error, which he immediately reported to the commanding officer. Lieutenant Nicol took charge of the bridge while a check was made. Land had not been visible since the last fix at Egg Island, so the ship's course was altered to northward, leading them toward land. The sea state had now increased to gale force and the wind had gone around to the west. Depth soundings were taken, and, by 1400, measurements placed the ship one mile north of Carousse Bank, east of Cape Canso.

The ship's course was now adjusted to 270 degrees, bringing it toward land. At 1630 the gyro compasses were again wandering and the course was altered to 270 degrees by magnetic compass. *Quinte* was shipping a considerable amount of water and because of defects to the bridge structure from the refit, water poured into the chart room over the depth-sounding machine. Attempts to repair the machine were made, but it could no longer be trusted for sounding, as it repeatedly broke down.[16]

On 29 November at 1105, *Quinte*'s course was altered to 040 degrees; land had not been sighted and the ship had now been steaming for almost 40 hours on what should have been a 27-hour transit. An hour later, *Quinte*'s radar became inoperable. She had now lost her radar, radios, compass, and depth sounder — it was as if she had been thrown back in time.

Navigation of the ship would now have to be done the "old-fashioned way." A very high sea was still making a solar sighting impracticable for longitude, but visibility had improved enough that a meridian sighting could be made for latitude. There was only one sextant aboard the ship, the personal property of the navigating officer. But as this delicate navigational tool was brought to the bridge, it was dropped to the deck. With no way of checking the sextant for errors, it too could no longer be relied upon.

Relief came at 1630 when land had finally been sighted; this was the first sighting since Egg Island. Identification of Louisburg and Louisburg Buoy were made, and at 2005 the ship rounded what was identified as Scateri Island. Just after 2100, *Quinte* had identified land considered to be Flint Island on her beam. Here she overtook an oil tanker and signalled for her name and destination. The ship identified herself as *Elkhound,* bound for Sydney.

Considerable snow flurries were now falling, making visibility difficult, and the compass could not be relied on, so the ship was steered by the white light thought to be Flat Point. At 2135 the officer-of-the-watch reported to Lieutenant Nicol, who had just stepped into the chart room, that the light thought to be Flat Point on Ciboux Island was too near. The commanding officer immediately came out to the bridge and ordered the ship stopped. Three minutes later, at 2138, Quinte grounded hard.

Both engines were immediately put to full astern. Several attempts were made using the engines to free the ship, and at 2145, aided by a swell, *Quinte* floated clear. Collision stations were immediately sounded on grounding, and all watertight doors closed and checked. The engineering officer reported the damage to *Quinte* as controllable. Contact with some nearby Fairmiles was made by projecting Quinte's searchlight onto the low clouds, and the ship proceeded away from the danger.[17]

The Fairmiles closed *Quinte* at 0200 and acquainted her with her position; the light they had misidentified and were following was actually the light to Horse Head Shoals, which they struck. Quinte proceeded to follow the Fairmile HMCS *Q093,* who acted as a guide. To assist *Quinte* in steering, a towline was passed from *Q093.* This did

Photo courtesy Walter Gregory.

HMCS Quinte, *partially submerged in St. Peter's Bay, Cape Breton, after striking Horse Head Shoal on 30 November 1942.*

Photo courtesy Walter Gregory.

A closer view of Quinte *partially submerged in St. Peter's Bay.*

not produce the desired results, so *Q093* placed her pilot, Captain Patrick Campbell, aboard *Quinte*, and tied herself along *Quinte*'s port quarter.

Proceeding slowly at two knots into St. Peter's Bay, the pilot suggested anchoring in five fathoms of water, but Lieutenant Nicol pressed for beaching the ship, as the fuel tanks were now empty and the boilers were out. The pumps couldn't run without the boilers and engines, and *Quinte* was still taking on water.

The tanker *Elkhound* had since entered the bay, and *Quinte* came alongside her to take on fuel and re-light the boilers. Once the two ships were together, though, the engineering officer reported the water had now flooded the boilers and consequently they couldn't be lighted. The lines were cast off from *Elkhound,* and *Quinte* drifted toward the beach with assistance from *Q093*.

Quinte eventually came to rest on the beach and settled in the water. The crew passed a line from her bow to the shore to secure the ship. Slowly, her stern settled and submerged in the water, and she developed a slight list, but none of her crew were injured and the ship did not appear to receive any further damage. She was secured by 0840 on 30 November 1942.

The storm that caused *Quinte* so much grief earlier had knocked out all telephone and telegraph communication on Cape Breton, and no communication was possible with Sydney to inform the local command of *Quinte*'s predicament.[18] The Fairmile sent a message to Halifax Command, informing them that *Quinte* was aground and required assistance, but the local command in Sydney could not locate her, so the RCMP was dispatched in patrol boats to locate the ship. Lieutenant Commander Wells, RCNR (engineer), representing the Naval Officer in Charge (NOIC) Sydney, Nova Scotia,[19] boarded *Quinte* on the afternoon of 30 November to inspect the ship and her situation.

Photo courtesy Walter Gregory.

Salvage operations were begun by the Foundation Maritime Ltd's ship, Foundation Aranmore.

Rescue and salvage operations commenced immediately. The armed yacht HMCS *Elk* arrived on scene escorting tugs, which tried to refloat *Quinte*, but they were too small and lacked the necessary power for the job.[20]

The salvage company Foundation Maritime Limited was engaged to refloat *Quinte*, and Captain Featherstone arrived on the scene by car on 3 December. One of the company's large ocean-going tugs, *Foundation Aranmore*, arrived on 5 December to commence operations, escorted by HMCS *Chedabucto*. Most of *Quinte*'s crew was sent back to Halifax, except for a small crew that remained with her to assist in the salvage of their ship, including the commanding officer, the engineer officer, a sub-lieutenant, six stokers, and six seamen.[21]

Despite *Quinte* being partially submerged, work proceeded very quickly and she was refloated 10 days later on 15 December. She was towed to the wall of St. Peter's Lock, the entrance to the Bras d'Or Lakes, to pump the remaining water from the ship.[22]

Unfortunately for *Quinte*, her string of misfortune was not yet finished. A second message was sent to Halifax from the salvage company, stating very simply, "On December 16th while being pumped she took a sudden and severe list and rolled away from the wall onto her side."[23] During pumping operations, the remaining water in *Quinte* shifted and she had rolled onto her side and capsized, this time sinking completely with only the side of her hull now visible.

No longer was this a simple task of refloating the ship; arrangements had to be made to secure her to large tackles and pull her upright. The weather was an added complication, as the water was now starting to freeze and the workers' greatest fear was that she would be iced-in while submerged. Because of the extended time required to salvage *Quinte*, she was decommissioned from the navy on 17 January 1943.

Photo courtesy Walter Gregory.

View of Quinte *after she has been patched and refloated. She will be towed to the wall of St. Peter's Canal to continue salvage operations.*

Photo courtesy Foundation Company of Canada and hazegray.org.

Quinte, *on her side, in the frozen canal. Lifting masts have been placed on the side of the canal to right the ship.*

Photo courtesy Foundation Company of Canada and hazegray.org.

Another view, this time from astern as Quinte *is broken free of the ice.*

Now the investigation and inquiries began. Eventually, a court martial was formed that listed several of *Quinte*'s officers who stood watch during the voyage as responsible for the initial grounding, including the commanding officer, navigating officer, and three others. The investigation found that the ship had actually steamed almost 500 miles when the trip should have taken 270. As in most cases of a court martial, the commanding officer was found to be primarily at fault for not ensuring his vessel was "in all respects ready for sea." The commanding officer should have refused to sail and ensured that his ship, equipment, and compasses were all working properly before departure. Also, when fuel could not be drawn from *Ungava* he should have signalled for another source.

The court martial board did not find Lieutenant Nicol solely at fault for the problems that affected his ship — the board also laid blame on the administrative side of the navy. The Senior Naval Officer (SNO) for Lunenburg was actually located in Liverpool, and had no easy way to travel to Lunenburg to observe the ship's refitting there. The board stated that it is the SNO's responsibility to ensure that all ships are given the time, stores, and facilities to ensure their ships are ready for sea. Similarly, the breakdown in communications led to the fuel message not reaching *Ungava*, causing *Quinte* to leave harbour with only partial tanks of fuel, all contributing to *Quinte* losing her equipment to breakdowns, running aground, and running out of fuel.[24]

Salvage work on the sunken *Quinte* took almost five months, both to right the ship and refloat her,[25] with operations ending on 24 April 1943 when she finally was taken in tow by the tug *Ocean Eagle*, first to Mulgrave and then to Pictou, Nova Scotia, on 25 April.[26] The total cost of salvaging was $135,000 and towing was an additional $4,564.83.[27]

Temporary repairs were made at Pictou to ensure the safety of the ship, and she was later moved

The Foundation-operated tug Ocean Eagle *(ex.* St. Arvans*) and* Foundation Scarboro *arrive to begin refloating* Quinte.

Quinte *now lies upright alongside the edge of the canal.*

Quinte *is now refloated.*

to the Pictou Foundry Company for refit, with an estimated cost of repairs at $350,000.[28] While in refit, the decision was made to send *Quinte* to Cornwallis as a training ship, adding additional anti-aircraft weapons to allow her to carry out duties as a gunnery training ship.

Work on *Quinte* was not completed until June 1944, and she was recommissioned into the RCN on 27 June. Quinte re-entered service under the temporary command of Lieutenant J.B.B. Morrow, RCN, and arrived at Halifax on 9 July 1944, where some final defects were corrected. She returned to operational service on 20 August 1944 and proceeded to Deep Brook, Nova Scotia, to assume her training duties with HMCS *Cornwallis*.[29]

There was finally the opportunity to celebrate aboard *Quinte*, when she hosted the christening ceremony of a newborn child of one of her officers, Lieutenant Shaw, and his wife, on 19 September 1944. Command of the ship was later passed to Skipper Lieutenant C.C. Clattenburg, RCNR, on 27 November 1944.

Quinte's trials, even in the final months of the war, were still not over. On 11 February 1945, she was secured to Pier 5 at Saint John, New Brunswick, while HMCS *Chicoutimi*, a Flower-class corvette, was tied alongside her and outboard. The corvette, being the larger ship, at 205 feet, extended past *Quinte*'s bow and stern and so was secured to both *Quinte* and the dock. At 0600 a swell began with a rising tide, and the two ships began to pound together.[30]

Quinte was protected from the swell and tide by the larger ship, but *Chicoutimi* continued to move and the two ships ground hard together. Fenders were hung between the ships but were either crushed or had their lines cut as the vessels collided. A tug was

Photo courtesy Canada Department of National Defence/Library and Archives Canada/PA-115630.

HMCS Quinte, *after reconstruction. Her minesweeping gear has been removed and her anti-aircraft weapons have been increased in order to serve as a gunnery training ship at Cornwallis. Deep Brook, Nova Scotia, 6 September 1944.*

then called in an attempt to separate the ships, but it didn't arrive until 1030. Until then, *Quinte*'s executive officer, engineer officer, and officer of the day could only watch as their ship bore the brunt of a pounding from the corvette.

Chicoutimi received only minor structural damage and was otherwise unaffected.[31] However, the same could not be said for *Quinte*: she had five of her structural support frames crushed and bent, the bulkhead in the seaman's mess was buckled, and a section of her deck plating would have to be replaced. Overall, *Quinte* was no longer seaworthy. Estimates for the repair were one week, at a cost of $1,200.[32] The damage was corrected in Saint John and she was then able to return to her duties as a gunnery training ship.

On 15 March 1945, Lieutenant D.C. MacPherson, RCNVR, took over command of *Quinte*. She remained in the Bay of Fundy and was still attached to *Cornwallis* when the war ended. Command of the ship changed to Lieutenant R.B. Taylor, RCNVR, on 20 July 1945.

Quinte returned to Halifax at the end of July 1945, where she was transferred to the Naval Research Establishment at Halifax. On 7 March 1946, she received her final commanding officer, Lieutenant L. McQuarrie, RCNVR. She continued in the role of a research ship for just over a year.

Quinte was paid off on 25 October 1946. The ship was sold to Halifax Shipyards Limited and broken up by the Dominion Steel Corporation at Sydney, Nova Scotia, in 1947.[33]

Ask any sailor and they will tell you that the heart and soul of a ship is her bell, and *Quinte*'s bell is proudly displayed in Belleville at the site of the local Sea Cadet Corps named for the ship, RCSCC Quinte.

AWARDS EARNED BY CREW

- George Cairns Ness, Commissioned Engineer, RCNR: Mention in Dispatches (MID)

  For exceptional keenness and devotion to duty over long periods at sea since the beginning of hostilities. This Officer has always maintained his engine room department so that its operational efficiency has been of the highest order, and no situation has ever arisen with which he was unable to cope. He is a cheerful and willing leader, inspiring confidence in his men.

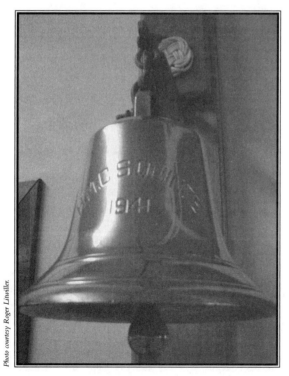

Photo courtesy Roger Litwiller.

The bell for HMCS Quinte *is kept by the Sea Cadet Corps that shares her name; RCSCC Quinte is located in Belleville, Ontario.*

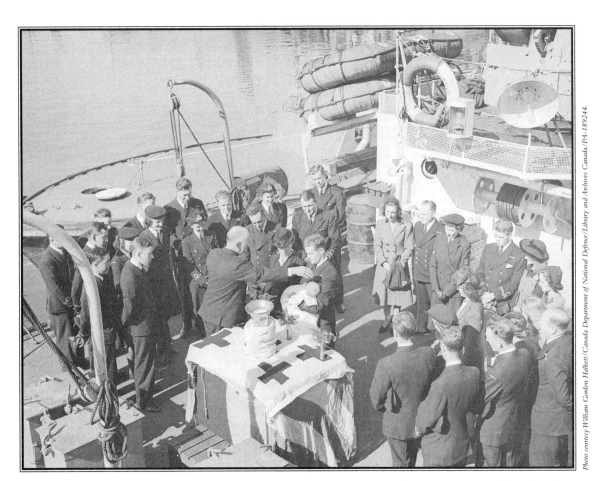

Photo courtesy William Gordon Halkett/Canada Department of National Defence/Library and Archives Canada/PA-189244.

Christening of child aboard HMCS Quinte, at Digby, Nova Scotia, on 19 September 1944. A storage locker draped with flags serves as an altar, Quinte's upturned bell is used as the christening basin, and shell casings from her guns are flower vases.

Commanding Officers

C.A. Nicol, LT, RCNR	30 August 1941 to 17 January 1943
I.B.B. Morrow, LT, RCN	10 November 1944 to 26 November 1944
C.C. Clattenburg, SKPR/LT, RCNR	27 November 1944 to 14 March 1945
D.C. MacPherson, LT, RCNVR	15 March 1945 to 19 July 1945
R.B. Taylor, LT, RCNVR	20 July 1945 to 3 August 1945
L. McQuarrie, LT, RCNR	7 March 1946 to 25 October 1946

**HMCS *QUINTE*
BATTLE HONOURS**

ATLANTIC   1941–1942

Specifications

Name:	HMCS *Quinte*, named for Bay of Quinte		
Classification:	Bangor-class minesweeper, 1939–1940 program		
Builder:	Burrard Dry Dock Company Limited — Vancouver, British Columbia		
Keel Laid: 14/12/40	Launched: 08/03/41	Commissioned: 30/08/41	Paid Off: 25/10/46
Length: 180 feet	Beam: 28 feet, 6 inches	Draught: 8 feet, 3 inches	
Displacement: 672 tons	Speed: 16 knots	Endurance: not available	Fuel: 143 tons
Crew: 6 officers, 77 other ranks	Machinery: two Admiralty 3 drum water tube boilers, two shafts, vertical triple expansion reciprocating engines		
Armament (as built):	- one 4 inch QF gun — forward gun platform - one 2-pdr. pom-pom MK VIII gun — after gun platform - two single .303 machine guns — bridge - two depth charge throwers — waist - one depth charge rail — stern - four depth charge chutes — stern - depth charges - minesweeping gear		
Post-refit (1944, as gunnery training ship):	- one 4 inch QF gun — forward gun platform - one 2-pdr. pom-pom MK VIII gun — after gun platform - two single .303 machine guns — bridge - one twin 20 mm Oerlikon machine gun — quarterdeck - two single 20 mm Oerlikon machine guns — aft - two depth charge throwers — waist - one depth charge rail — stern - four depth charge chutes — stern - one depth charge trap - 10 depth charges		

Specifications of HMCS Quinte.

Chart prepared by Roger Litwiller.

CHAPTER 6

HMCS *Quinte* (II)
149
Bay Class
Minesweeper

Photo courtesy RCSCC Quinte.

HMCS Quinte *(II) commissioned on 15 October 1954.*

THE SECOND *QUINTE* WAS THE longest-serving ship of the six ships named after the Bay of Quinte area. She was designed during the Korean War and built after the Armistice. Her design incorporated hard lessons learned during the Second World War and in Korea, and she would serve during the Cold War.

Canada still had a need for ships with minesweeping capabilities. Although the approaches to Halifax had been mined only once during the war, it had been proved it could be done, and with technology leaping ahead, mines were an inexpensive weapon to either defend or attack a port or waterway anywhere in the world.

HMCS *Quinte* (II) was a Bay-class minesweeper and one of the 14 minesweepers built during the 1950 and 1951 programs to replace the aging Bangor class from the Second World War. All of the Bay-class minesweepers were given names for bays; her name was chosen to continue the line of the first *Quinte*,[1] allowing the newer ship to claim all battle honours earned by the original.

Quinte *under construction at the Port Arthur Shipbuilding Company Limited.*

Her keel was laid on 14 June 1952 at the Port Arthur Shipbuilding Company in Port Arthur, Ontario, now part of Thunder Bay. The ship was constructed extensively of wood, aluminum, and non-magnetic alloys to allow her to sweep mines triggered by a ship's magnetic field without detonating them herself. As the wise saying goes, "Any ship can be a minesweeper, once!"

Quinte was a new kind of minesweeper based on a Royal Navy design converted for use by Canada. Her hull was made of wood, but the remainder of the ship was constructed of aluminum, both for strength and to save weight. The savings in weight allowed for better comfort for the men who would sail in her. It was now possible to have a central mess for dining instead of having to carry your meal from the galley to your mess. Also, the men were given spacious lockers for personal gear and moved from hammocks slung from the deckhead to bunks with a mattress. Canadian manufacturers and shipbuilders had to come up with new materials, building techniques, and methods to produce these new ships.[2]

Photo courtesy Thunder Bay Historical Museum Society.

Mrs. J.B. Caldwell christening Quinte *on 8 August 1952.*

Quinte's christening ceremony took place on 8 August 1953 and was sponsored by Mrs. J.B. Caldwell, the wife of Captain J.B. Caldwell, MBE, RCN, assistant chief of naval technical services (ships). Mrs. Caldwell broke the bottle of champagne across *Quinte*'s bows and spoke these simple words: "I Christen this ship 'Quinte.' May God bless her and all who sail in her." With that most important blessing, given to ships for centuries, *Quinte* slipped into the cold water of Lake Superior.[3]

After the ceremony, a luncheon held by the shipbuilding company was attended by over 300 employees, friends, civic officials, and members of the RCN. Mr. R. Lowery, president of the company, announced that with *Quinte*'s completion the yard would commence to built a third minesweeper for the Canadian Navy. During his speech, Mr. Lowery had these words to say about the minesweepers:

I am sometimes angered by critics who point to the smallness of the ship and the time and money spent to build it. No one who knew the facts would criticize. Whether you are a shipbuilder or not you must admit the ship is not big or impressive. Those who witnessed the launching at the yard probably noticed a Paterson Steamship Lines boat being built which is 50 times as big in terms of displacement. Similarly

Quinte is launched into the cold water of Lake Superior.

in Quebec yards at the present time two ships are being built of 40,000 tons displacement. You must remember that the safety of those ships depends upon the readiness, efficiency and skilful handling of the ships, one we launched today.[4]

The ship was accepted by the RCN and commissioned 15 October 1954 in a ceremony with Commodore W.L. M. Brown, assistant chief of naval staff (air), representing naval headquarters,[5] and Commander (E) R.J. Craig, representing the assistant chief of naval technical services (ships).[6]

Her first commanding officer was Lieutenant Commander Daniel Patrick Brownlow, CD, RCN. Lieutenant Commander Brownlow was born in Northern Ireland and joined the Royal Canadian Navy Volunteer Reserve at Edmonton in 1939 as an ordinary seaman. He served in the North Atlantic in HMCS *Annapolis* and was promoted to commissioned rank in 1943. He also served a tour in HMCS *Huron* in Korean waters.[7]

With the ceremonies complete and her crew in place, *Quinte* departed Port Arthur on 16 October 1954, sailing into the clear waters of Lake Superior in transit to Montreal. She had been underway for only one and a half hours when at 1610 the crew

Quinte *under trials in Lake Superior.*

was called to stations, as a fire had broken out in the heater boiler in the main engine room. The fire was contained quickly and extinguished by the crew. Damage was confined to the boiler and stack, but the ship had to return to Port Arthur for repairs. The decision was made to allow the manufacturer of the boiler, located in Montreal, to investigate the cause of the fire and repair the damage. This meant *Quinte* would have to sail through the Lakes in late autumn weather without heat for the crew spaces, and, once a quantity of electric heaters were purchased in Port Arthur, the ship departed once again.[8]

Quinte's departure and subsequent fire was over-shadowed in the Canadian media as Hurricane Hazel was just beginning to slam into Southern Ontario that same day, causing flooding, severe damage, and many deaths.

Late in October 1954, *Quinte* was attached to HMCS *Scotian*, the naval reserve unit in Halifax, as a training ship. Regularly, she would be attached to the First Canadian Minesweeping Squadron for mine-sweeping exercises. The Bay-class minesweepers were of an ideal size and design to train junior naval officers in ship handling and sea keeping. She also participated

Photo courtesy Thunder Bay Historical Museum Society.

Ceremonies in Thunder Bay for the newly commissioned HMCS Quinte *on 15 October 1954. Commodore W.L.M. Brown, assistant chief of naval staff (air), is standing behind the desk.*

in the training of University Naval Training Division (UNTD) cadets, men, and the Women's Royal Naval Service (WRNS or Wrens).

While attached to HMCS *Scotian*, a typical month would find *Quinte* at sea for about eight days and in harbour for the remainder. During February 1955, she was given over to the National Film Board of Canada for a day so they could produce a film demonstrating minesweeping.[9]

The following month, *Quinte* was attached to the First Canadian Minesweeping Flotilla for the first of many trips south for exercises and workups in the Caribbean. She was joined by her sister ships of the flotilla: *Gaspe*, *Trinity*, and *Ungava*. The training cruise lasted from March through most of April, and calls were paid by the ships to St. John's, Antigua, Montserrat, and Bridgetown, Barbados. *Quinte*'s crew formed an armed guard during wreath-laying ceremonies at Port-au-Prince, Haiti, and this was followed by a four-day visit to Nassau in the Bahamas.

The flotilla then sailed for Charleston, South Carolina, for a three-day exercise with minesweepers from the United States Navy, then on to three days of training at the Mine Warfare School at Yorktown, Virginia.[10] The training exercises in the Caribbean and southern United States would become a yearly routine for *Quinte* and were highly anticipated by her crew.

On 7 June 1956, *Quinte* was assigned to assist with "Bluenose Days," the celebration of the newly launched ferry service from Bar Harbour, Maine, to Yarmouth in the Bay of Fundy. The festivities were named after the new ferry MV *Bluenose*. *Quinte* was to rendezvous with the ferry and the destroyer HMCS *Huron* and take station ahead of *Bluenose* to escort her into Yarmouth Harbour.

Unfortunately, *Bluenose* soon overtook *Quinte*, who then followed the ferry into harbour. Lieutenant Commander Brownlow describes the scene that greeted his ship best:

> Traffic in the harbour was uncontrolled. A number of trawlers gaily decorated both with flags and people milled about in company with other craft. These water "hot rods" with sirens screaming proceeded to carry out their own version of the game of "chicken" with MV *Bluenose* and HMCS *Quinte*.

He went on to add:

> The situation began to assume the proportions of an old time movie. Among the din and the roar of sirens, bands and plain old fashion yelling, I strongly suspect our attempts to make proper sound signals in compliance with "The Rules" branded us as good sports for getting into the spirit of things.

While *Quinte* *was* attempting to safely navigate through the congestion of the harbour, one of the local fishermen must have realized Lieutenant Commander Brownlow's frustration, for he called over and explained, "You know how it is Sir, we're having a bit of a celebration today."[11]

On 1 October 1956, *Quinte* was involved in a collision with HMCS *Portage*, an Algerine-class minesweeper, at No. 5 jetty in the Halifax dockyards. *Quinte* was secured to the jetty with HMCS *Sault Ste. Marie* ahead of her when *Portage* approached the two ships to secure alongside *Sault Ste. Marie*. A head rope was passed between the two ships, when a wash could be seen from the stern of *Portage*, indicating her starboard propeller was turning astern. It was observed that *Portage*'s stern was turning into *Sault Ste. Marie* and it appeared the two ships would collide. Then *Portage* proceeded directly astern, narrowly clearing *Sault Ste. Marie* and heading directly toward the bow of *Quinte* while gaining speed. With *Quinte* secured to the jetty, Lieutenant Commander Brownlow could only watch with a feeling of frustration and helplessness as *Portage* collided with his

ship. Almost immediately, *Portage* pulled ahead and then secured alongside *Sault Ste. Marie*.[12]

Damage to the two ships was minor, with *Quinte* receiving damage to her stem and *Portage* damaging her stern plates, guard rails, and ensign staff.[13] The board of inquiry found all responsibility for the collision with *Portage*, specifically with the engineering officer, who was not in the engine room while his ship was entering harbour, contrary to regulations.[14]

In January 1957, *Quinte*, along with *Gaspe*, *Trinity*, *Ungava*, and *Resolute*, visited Charleston, South Carolina, for exercises. Later, in February, they

Port-side view of HMCS Quinte *(II).*

travelled to San Juan, Puerto Rico, and Bermuda for similar purposes.

On 3 March 1957, while alongside in Halifax, the steering alarm rang in *Quinte*'s wheelhouse at 2050. Able Seaman Gerber, the quartermaster on duty, turned off all main steering switches. On further investigation, he noticed smoke coming out of the tiller flat and stood by with a fire extinguisher. The fire department was called and arrived on scene along with *Fire Tug #1*. Fire crews entered the compartment and found the electric steering motor had been burnt, which was caused by an overload. Damage to the ship was confined to the motor by

the quick actions of the duty watch and repairs would cost an estimated $185.[15]

On 13 June 1957, while alongside in Halifax, *Quinte* received a radio message at 0930 notifying her of an imminent air raid. The ship was at one-hour notice for steam, but managed to leave the jetty in less than fifteen minutes with main armament manned, ammunition provided, all hands at their stations, and the entire ship at the highest state of readiness and prepared for any emergency.

It would turn out that the message was an error, and *Quinte* returned to the jetty by 0955 and stood down. But this simple error had reminded her crew

HS-53255. Photo courtesy National Defence Imaging Library.

First Minesweeping Squadron under command of Commander. A.C. Campbell at jetty in St. Pierre, Miquelon, on 17 June 1958.

of the staunch realism of the Cold War, and they inadvertently found out that they were capable of rising to any occasion.[16]

As Lieutenant Commander Brownlow's command of *Quinte* ended, on 23 June 1957, he concluded his final report as commanding officer: "In farewell I would say to my successor, I leave a stout ship, a first class ship's company and the hope he will enjoy his appointment as I have enjoyed mine."[17]

Quinte's next commanding officer was Lieutenant Commander Reginald Philip Mylrea, CD, RCN, of North Battleford and Regina, Saskatchewan.

He entered the Royal Canadian Naval Volunteer Reserve in 1933 and transferred to the RCN in 1937 as an ordinary seaman. In addition to several shore postings, he served in various destroyers, frigates, and a cruiser. Lieutenant Commander Mylrea was well-known in boxing circles, having won the Golden Gloves Intermediate Championship in 1936.[18]

HMCS *Loon* took over as tender to HMCS *Scotian* on 12 March 1957, and *Quinte* was permanently assigned to the First Canadian Minesweeping Flotilla. She would remain with the flotilla for the rest of her career.

HS-53282. Photo courtesy National Defence Imaging Library.

First Minesweeping Squadron in close formation off Gaspe Bay coast on 17 June 1958. HMCS Quinte *is second on left.*

On 15 October 1957, *Quinte* entered HMC Dockyard at Halifax for her first refit and would remain there until completed on 7 January 1957. During this time, almost her entire crew was transferred to other ships, except for one officer and seven men. Later in the month, *Quinte* proceeded to the Virgin Islands for a welcomed training period and workups for her new crew.[19]

Training and exercises are meant to prepare the ship and her crew for any eventuality, and *Quinte* was put to that test when, on 18 March 1957, she received orders to proceed and assist in the search for a missing aircraft. The craft in question was an avenger from VS-881 Squadron, from the RCN Naval Air Station HMCS *Shearwater*. A general recall was sent out and *Quinte* slipped her lines in 20 minutes with all her officers and 85 percent of her crew. She was joined in the search by HMCS *Haida*, *Fundy*, and *Granby*, as well as several aircraft. Unfortunately, after two days the search was called off, having failed to discover any evidence of the missing aircraft.[20]

Later in the year, *Quinte* was joined by *Resolute* at the annual Nova Scotia Fisheries Exhibition in Lunenburg, where the crews took part in all the festivities. On 14 September 1957, a major fire broke out in the town at 0500, demolishing the Legion Hall and two dwellings. *Quinte's* executive officer, along with fifteen men, went down to assist the firefighters.[21]

Two months later, on 18 November 1957, *Quinte* was sent for her second refit, at the hands of Purdy Brothers Marine Engineers. The refit was completed on 27 February 1958, and on 30 March 1958, while alongside in Dartmouth, Nova Scotia, *Quinte* was the scene of a large christening ceremony. In a service officiated by Command Chaplain Bruce Peglar and Chaplain W.G. Bingham, 14 children of sailors and naval personnel were baptized, ranging in age from 1 to 31.[22] This marks one of the largest ceremonies of its kind to be held aboard a Canadian naval ship.[23]

On 16 February 1959, *Quinte* was once again sailing for Bermuda after completing another refit. The transit south was characterized by high seas and hurricane-force winds. She came alongside at Ireland Island on the 20th and spent the next eight days cleaning ship.[24]

The next day, on 21 February, some of the crew were returning to the ship from leave, when one of the cooks, Petty Officer Orville Earl Guest of London, Ontario, witnessed an accident involving a sailor from the gate vessel, HMCS *Porte Saint-Jean*. He saw the sailor fall overboard, strike his head on the jetty, and land in the water between the vessel and the dock. Guest dove in and held the unconscious man's head above water, while fending off the vessel from the jetty with his body until he could be assisted by other members of the crew, and both men were hauled to safety.[25]

For his actions, Petty Officer Guest would be recommended for the Queen's Commendation for Bravery. The award was presented on 12 June 1959 with the following citation: "There is no doubt that had not Petty Officer Guest taken this timely action in this dangerous situation, the Able Seaman would have drowned."[26]

While returning to Halifax, *Quinte* developed a defect in her port main engine clarifier tank, which required her to be taken into dockyard hands when she arrived on 3 May 1959. The defect was repaired in 4 days and *Quinte* returned to service.[27]

HMCS Quinte *(149) at anchor on Gaspe Bay Harbour, 17 June 1958.*

On 17 June 1959, *Quinte* slipped from Halifax with her squadron and proceeded to Gaspé to join the escort for the Royal Yacht *Britannia*. She was to be escorted up the St. Lawrence to convey Her Majesty Queen Elizabeth and President Dwight D. Eisenhower to open the newly constructed St. Lawrence Seaway. However, two hours out of Halifax, *Quinte* developed a defect in her port main engine and was forced to return to harbour for repairs,

rendering her unable to take part in this historic event. The repairs were completed on 25 July 1959.[28]

Quinte was able to participate with the other ships of her squadron on 28 July, however, when they secured head to stern in Halifax Harbour with the other ships of the Atlantic Command. They remained drawn up to greet Her Majesty when she arrived on the 31st and to bid her farewell on 1 August. The next day, in honour of the royal visit, the ships

HS-53283. Photo courtesy National Defence Imaging Library.

spliced the main brace and the commanding officer of *Quinte* reported, "the ceremony was carried out with its usual enthusiasm."[29]

On 2 September 1959, Lieutenant Commander Mylrea stepped down as commanding officer. *Quinte's* third commanding officer, Lieutenant Commander R.J. Paul, CD, RCN, took command of the ship the following day.

The First Canadian Minesweeping Flotilla departed Halifax on 10 October 1959 for a visit to Albany, New York, requiring the ships to travel the 160-mile passage up the Hudson River. The crews spent the trip watching the picturesque scenery from the rails as they passed the fine colonial-style mansions along the river's banks. Many small craft would come out from the yacht clubs dotted along the river, and people would line the shore and the bridges, waving at the flotilla as the ships sailed up the river. Some amusement was gained during an exchange of whistle signals between the ships of the flotilla and the trains of the New York Central Railway.

The first night found the flotilla berthed at West Point, the United States Army academy, commanding the heights of the west bank of the river. The flotilla

First Canadian Minesweeping Squadron dressed for Regatta, 4 July 1958. HMCS Chaleur *is in foreground.*

DNS-21190. Photo courtesy National Defence Imaging Library.

HS-59348. Photo courtesy National Defence Imaging Library.

HMCS Quinte *(149) entering West Point quay with bluffs of Hudson River in background, 12 October 1959.*

slipped their lines the next morning for the second day of travel along the Hudson River, this section even more scenic because of the narrowness of the river, and arrived in Albany at 1700 that afternoon to receive an ardent welcome. Every fire engine the city could spare was lined up on the docks with their hoses trained over the river. *Resolute* was first to proceed to her berth, but, as the ship approached the dock, the order to switch off the water hoses was not given, soaking *Resolute*'s bridge and everyone in it with fountains of water at 100 pounds pressure.

Nothing was spared: the crew, charts, logs, signals, and everything else were doused with water.[30]

Quinte was soon sent for another refit, from 9 November 1959 to 22 January 1960 in the shipyards of Lunenburg Foundry and Engineering Limited in Nova Scotia. On completion of refit, she returned to Halifax to take aboard stores and equipment. Unfortunately, as *Quinte* approached the seaward defence jetty she bumped it with her stem. A quick survey of the situation revealed that she had incurred considerable damage to her bow. Lieutenant

EKS-392, Photo courtesy National Defence Imaging Library.

First Minesweeping Squadron berthed at St. Pierre, Miquelon, inboard to outboard: HMC Ships Fundy, Chignecto, Resolute, Gaspe, Quinte, *and* Thunder.

Commander Paul, *Quinte*'s commanding officer, noted that the damage seemed to be out of proportion to the force of the bump. Further inspection revealed that the wooden stem under the metal cutwater was powdery from dry rot. Repairs to *Quinte* would lay her up again, until 14 April 1960.[31]

On 25 November 1960, *Quinte*'s crew was once again called to emergency stations, this time when a fire was reported in the engine room while at Halifax. The duty watch entered the engine room

and attacked the fire with portable CO_2 extinguishers from *Quinte* and the adjoining ships. When this did not suppress the fire, the watch closed off the engine room and activated the CO_2 flooding system. An hour later, the fire was extinguished except for a large mass of molten metal now lying in the bottom of the boiler's fire box. The cause of the fire was suspected to be a malfunction of the oil burner controls for the boiler. Damage was confined to the fire box, melting the boiler tubing, charring the pipe lagging on the exhaust trunking, and melting the insulation from nine overhead cables.[32] The boiler was no longer able to provide heat to the ship, so once again a quantity of electric heaters were acquired and installed to heat the crew compartments and keep *Quinte* operational until repairs could be made.[33]

January 1961 found *Quinte* preparing for her annual trip to the Caribbean. She spent a total of nine days at St. George's, Bermuda, accompanied by *Thunder* and *Chaleur*. All three ships returned to Halifax on 16 January, and at the end of the month *Quinte* proceeded to Liverpool, Nova Scotia, for her annual refit, this time at the Steel and Engine Products Limited wharf. She returned to service after completing engine trials and returned to Halifax on 17 March 1961.[34]

Quinte made her return to the Great Lakes and freshwater of her beginnings in May of 1961. She was joined by her entire squadron, and the first ports of call were Quebec City and Montreal. The squadron entered the Lakes through the St. Lawrence Seaway, where *Quinte* had missed the opening ceremony due to engine defects. Together they traversed Lake Ontario and paid a visit to Port Stanley in Lake Erie after passing through the Welland Canal.

The squadron left Port Stanley on 1 June 1961 and reached Sarnia the next day on the St. Clair River and Lake Huron. During this time, more than 3,000 people visited the ships and cruises were laid on to take out various school representatives. When it came time to close the gangway and secure the ship to visitors, it was discovered that the line of people still waiting was over a block long, so the time of visiting was extended by two hours.

The squadron steamed into Port Arthur on 7 June 1961. *Quinte* had returned to her place of birth, along with *Thunder*, both ships having been constructed at the Port Arthur Shipbuilding Company. Also present were *Fundy*, *Resolute*, *Chaleur*, and *Chignecto*.

They were to remain in Thunder Bay for four days, and during this time several cruises were laid on for dignitaries, reservists, and the local schools. Demonstrations were given showing the minesweepers' ability to work as a squadron and perform minesweeping exercises. To quote the local newspaper, "All heartily agreed when the trip was over they were henceforth converted fans of the First Canadian Minesweeping Squadron."[35]

The group departed Thunder Bay and returned to Lake Huron, where they split up. *Quinte* and *Chignecto* proceeded together to Georgian Bay for a visit to Meaford, Ontario. The two ships were met with great enthusiasm by the town, and the crews repaid this hospitality by marching in a parade and taking more than 600 residents on three short harbour cruises.[36]

The two ships left Meaford for Sarnia on the 14th and rejoined the other ships from the squadron two days later at Port Stanley. They made their way out of the Great Lakes for Montreal and returned home, reaching Halifax on 30 June 1961.

Quinte received her fourth commanding officer on 3 August 1961, when Lieutenant Commander G.G. Armstrong, RCN, took command of the ship.

For the remainder of the year, *Quinte* continued with her normal role of training and minesweeping exercises, as well as visits to Newfoundland, Charleston, Philadelphia, New York City, Bermuda, and Connecticut.

In March 1962, *Quinte* landed ammunition and stores for refit and went onto the Dartmouth Marine Slips. The refit would last until 3 April and cost $55,000.[37]

On 22 May 1962, the First Canadian Mine-sweeping Squadron departed Halifax for their second trip into the Great Lakes. The first two ports of call were Quebec City and Montreal. Only two ships were required for the next stop, Oshawa, on Lake Ontario, so *Quinte* and the remainder of the squadron proceeded west to Clarkson for fuel. Later, on 2 June, the entire squadron joined together for a four-day visit to Toronto. While in Ontario's capital, the squadron provided cruises on the lake to dignitaries.

CS-554. Photo courtesy National Defence Imaging Library.

The six units of First Canadian Minesweeping Squadron nest on HMCS Cape Scott *in Shelburne Harbour. Included are* Chaleur *(164),* Fundy *(159), and* Quinte *(149).*

Photo courtesy Maritime Command Museum, Halifax.

Units of the First Canadian Minesweeping Squadron proceed to sea in arrowhead formation, bound for NATO exercise "Sweep Clear Eight." Clockwise from top are HMC Ships Quinte *(149),* Fundy *(159),* Thunder *(161),* Chignecto *(160) and* Resolute *(154).*

The next port was Hamilton, where the squadron provided cruises and gave a large minesweeping demonstration in the harbour. *Quinte* and *Thunder* were detached from the group at this time for a weekend visit to the city of Oswego, New York.

Eventually, the two ships rejoined the others to transit the Welland Canal into Lake Erie and in turn visited Windsor, Sarnia, and Port Arthur. While in Port Arthur, the squadron participated in the opening of the new Keefer Lakehead Terminal. Following the ceremony, *Quinte* and *Thunder* sailed on a minesweeping demonstration in the approaches to the new terminal.

The minesweepers left Port Arthur on 24 June and, save for a fuel stop in Sarnia, headed straight out of the Lakes. After a brief stop in Montreal and Quebec City, the squadron returned to Halifax on 3 July 1962. This was the last trip *Quinte* made to the Great Lakes.[38]

Quinte, being the smallest of the six ships named for the Bay of Quinte area and having a shallow draft, would have been the only one able to visit the communities along the bay. Unfortunately, she was not scheduled to visit her namesake bay or the people of this area.

October 1962 found the squadron participating in exercise "Sweep Clear VII." The exercise was delayed by the approach of Hurricane Daisy, and the ships had to divert to the Straits of Canso to remain alongside the waiting wall for the locks until the weather cleared. On 13 October the exercise commenced, but the ships were again forced into Sydney due to poor weather. The next day the exercise was able to begin, and following a 42-hour period of continuous minesweeping, the group returned to Sydney and Halifax on 16 October.

Early in October, there was a marked increase in Soviet submarine contacts in the Atlantic. In response, Rear Admiral Kenneth Dyer, Flag Officer Atlantic Coast, increased the long-range patrols of the Argus aircraft. The increased patrols paid off when on 17 October an aircraft picked up a solid submarine contact 225 miles southeast of Halifax.

HMCS Quinte *(II) during* Cancominron *(I), 29 April 1963.*

Over the next few days, Canadian and American air and surface units would make several contacts with Soviet surface and submarine vessels.

On 22 October the world would suddenly take a drastic change as President Kennedy announced that nuclear missiles were being constructed on the Caribbean island of Cuba. With that announcement, the U.S. military went on alert at the DEFCON 3 level. A blockade of the island by U.S. naval forces was to commence on 24 October.

Our government had entered into an agreement of shared defence with the Americans, and if one country increased its defence level the other country was obligated to match them. Diefenbaker wavered in his decision and refused to place the Canadian military on alert.

On 23 October a fleet of Soviet ships was spotted heading toward Cuba and the American blockade. On the 24th, when the fleet was still heading toward Cuba, the American Strategic Air Command and some U.S. naval forces went to DEFCON 2: immediate enemy attack expected. Still, the Canadian military was not placed on alert. The prime minister finally agreed to place only the Canadian units assigned to the shared Northern Air Defence (NORAD) forces on an increased level of alert. This decision did not mention the Royal Canadian Navy.

Rear Admiral Dyer and naval headquarters in Ottawa knew we had commitments under the agreements with the U.S., and our naval forces had trained and practised for this very situation with U.S. Naval Forces for years, but without an order from the prime minister the fleet could not be brought to an alert for war. The solution came from Admiral Dyer, who as flag officer Atlantic Coast could order the East Coast Fleet to exercise at any time, without approval from naval headquarters or Ottawa.

By 26 October, Canada's naval forces were taking station in the North Atlantic, and ships and aircraft were at the ready with full war loads of ammunition and supplies. The entire East Coast Fleet was mobilized and Halifax Harbor was emptied. Since the lessons learned at Pearl Harbour, no fleet commander would allow his ships to be trapped in harbour with war imminent. Two alternate ports were set up with provisions, ammunition, and supplies at Shelburne and Sydney.

Quinte and her sister, *Chaleur*, were sent to Corner Brook, Newfoundland, on 25 October.[39]

Our navy contributed the aircraft carrier HMCS *Bonaventure* with 28 aircraft, as well as 13 destroyers, 9 frigates, 2 submarines, 6 minesweepers, 12 land-based tracker aircraft, and 32 Argus long-range patrol aircraft. The fleet patrolled the North Atlantic from Frobisher Bay to areas east of Boston, New York, Washington, and as far south as Norfolk, Virginia. Argus aircraft patrolled 600 miles out into the Atlantic as far as the Azores.

The American forces had commitments in the Pacific and Mediterranean and were therefore spread thin in the Atlantic. This meant Canada had more ready forces in the Atlantic than the Americans did.

On 28 October the world breathed a sigh of relief as the Soviet president appeared to back down and agreed to remove the missiles from Cuba. The U.S. suspended the blockade of Cuba, but kept all ships on station and at full alert. Although the political situation had changed, there was no evidence of change in the Soviet military posture.

On 29 October, *Quinte* and *Chaleur* were ordered to return to Halifax. On the return trip, the two ships encountered severe weather and *Quinte*'s workboat was carried away and damaged from water coming over the weather side of the ship. She was forced to remain in Halifax for repairs and maintenance.[40]

The crisis was finally over on 12 November, and our fleet returned to Halifax. The naval secretary summed up the entire Cuban crisis in a single sentence in his monthly report to Naval Headquarters: "Squadron Commanders and Commanding Officers have, almost without exception, commented on the value of the training obtained during the Cuban Crisis."[41]

During the standoff between the United States and Russia/Cuba, Canada's East Coast Fleet played an active role in submarine patrols of the North Atlantic. To give some perspective on the flurry of activities, in the preceding four years Canadian forces made a total of 66 contacts with Soviet submarines: four contacts in 1958, 19 in 1959, 21 in 1960, and 22 in 1961. During the 24 days of operations surrounding the Cuban Missile Crisis, from 23 October to 15 November 1962, Canadian forces had 136 submarine contacts.

Operations for the East Coast Fleet returned to normal just as quickly as they had mobilized, and on 13 November *Quinte* left Halifax to assist the auxiliary ship CNAV *Eastore* in laying mines for exercise "SWEEPEX 1/62," scheduled to begin the next day.

The first two weeks of January 1963 found *Quinte* in Halifax performing maintenance, and the ship was surveyed to prepare a list of defects for her upcoming refit. February had the squadron outside of Canadian waters with its annual trip to Bermuda, followed by minesweeping training at Charleston and a visit to New York City. The squadron then returned to Halifax on 6 March 1963.

Quinte again entered refit on 3 June 1963, at the Steel and Engine Products Limited in Liverpool, Nova Scotia. Eight days later the ship was moved onto the company's slips. Lieutenant Commander Armstrong wrote of the experience of getting *Quinte* onto the slips as "a very seamanlike if somewhat hair raising evolution accomplished using the Mersey river current, a Cape Island boat and skillful handling of the cradle."

The refit took longer than expected, and Lieutenant Commander Armstrong reported later that the quality of the work was high but completion of the refit was held up by "delay in supply of spares, shortage of skilled labour in the area and a limited work area for the amount of work to be done …"

The refit was completed 26 July 1963, and *Quinte* was undocked from the slip with the same degree of hazards as when she went onto the slips six weeks prior (unfortunately, Armstrong's report doesn't specifically list these hazards, though it is possible that the river current made it difficult to turn the ship 90 degrees to the shore). Lieutenant Commander Armstrong considered that his ship was placed "in jeopardy with no way of helping herself."

A single fishing boat had been used as a substitute tugboat to assist *Quinte* from the slip, and Armstrong recommended that a second tug should be used in the future to ensure the safety of the ship.[42]

Following completion of sea trials, Lieutenant Commander Armstrong stepped down from command of *Quinte*. Lieutenant Commander R.L. Donaldson, CD, RCN, took over command of the ship the following day, 30 July 1963.

In October 1963, *Quinte* joined the squadron in the Bay of Chaleur for a week of sea training called "Chaleur Bay Sweepex." The squadron then replenished from Dalhousie, New Brunswick, and on completion of the exercise *Quinte* departed in company with *Chaleur*.

The two ships sailed in a loose formation about five miles apart, with orders to investigate all contacts. *Quinte* and *Chaleur* sailed across the Gulf of St. Lawrence and then entered the open Atlantic through the Cabot Strait. While in the gulf, the two ships intercepted 13 contacts, but they found little traffic on the open ocean.

Quinte ended 1963 participating in exercise "Boat Cloak," staged off Isle Madame on the southern corner of Cape Breton Island. The 10-day exercise involved 20 ships from Atlantic Command, aircraft from HMCS *Shearwater*, and 200 soldiers from Camp Gagetown in New Brunswick. *Quinte*'s participation was typical of large exercises, with long periods of "nothing to do" broken up with "brief spasms of furious activity."[43] Her primary activities were exactly what she and her crew were trained for: laying, tending, and recovering Dan buoys.

Following Christmas and New Year's Eve, 1964 began with *Quinte* performing routine maintenance in preparation for engine trials on 10 January.

HS-59366. Photo courtesy National Defence Imaging Library.

HMCS Quinte *(II) abeam of HMCS* Resolute, *19 October 1959.*

Following the trials, the First Canadian Minesweeping Squadron was to assemble for the annual voyage to Bermuda and to depart on the 13th. Unfortunately, they were in for bad news: an announcement by the government on 8 January called for fleet reductions in order to lower operation and maintenance costs. Included in this was the paying off of the Bay-class minesweepers into reserve. With this announcement, all preparations for sea were cancelled and each ship in turn was given a decommissioning date; *Quinte* was the fifth of six minesweepers to be paid off.

Lieutenant Commander Donaldson wrote in his monthly report:

> [T]he long-delayed assemblage of the First Minesweeping Squadron and its final restoration as a fully worked-up unit of the fleet, with this ship in open competition for available honours, this

time was one of high optimism and well-defined purpose. The receipt of CANGEN 2 on 8 January, with its news of Fleet reduction, was a disappointment which can only be appreciated by those too absorbed in their work to be able to read the already-legible writing on the wall.[44]

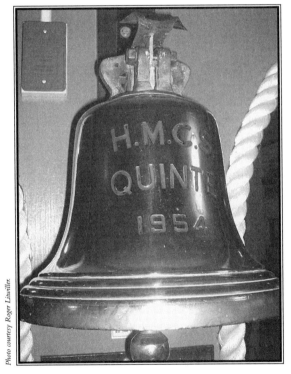

Photo courtesy Roger Litwiller.

The bell of HMCS Quinte *(II) is on display at the Bay of Quinte Yacht Club at 8 Wing/Canadian Forces Base Trenton, Ontario.*

A dinner party was held on 31 January 1964, marking the end of the First Canadian Minesweeping Squadron, and Lieutenant Commander Donaldson

ended his monthly report with, "On a more formal level, the calls of minesweeping Commanding Officers on the Flag Officer Atlantic Coast on 30 January, and the return call the next day, heralded the final dispersal. For all the funereal atmosphere of these affairs, the willingness of the Admiral to find time to attend was a source of encouragement."[45]

Quinte's service with the Royal Canadian Navy ended on 26 February 1964, when she was decommissioned and paid off. She was sold for disposal to Nova Holdings Limited of Halifax for $51,967.25 on 26 July 1966. The reason for the purchase was not known, but *Quinte* was later broken up.[46]

The first *Quinte*, being of wartime construction, was not in service long enough to receive a ship's badge. *Quinte* (II) was the first of the two ships, and the only one of the Bay of Quinte ships, to be assigned a badge. The badge itself is set in the round shape of Royal Canadian Navy Ships, with the Naval Crown at the head and three maple leafs at the bottom to signify the badge is Canadian.

The origin of the name *Quinte* is obscure, but *Quintus* in Latin is "fifth" and *quint* is "five." We use the word *quintet*, meaning "a group of five." Therefore the ship's name is broken down as *Quint-E* or five *E*s.

The Blazon of *Quinte's* badge is set on a green background with a Tudor rose, barbed and seeded in the centre, with five petals. The rose signifies the first settlers in the Bay of Quinte area and Prince Edward County, who were United Empire Loyalists. Surrounding the Tudor rose is a pentagonal cross pattee, the arms of which are formed by five letter *E*s, each letter facing the centre point of the rose. The ship's colours are white and green.

Although the badge was designed for the second *Quinte*, under the rules of heraldry the badge can be used for all ships of the same name and lineage, and therefore can be used for the first *Quinte*.

Quinte (II) was designed for minesweeping duties but found herself performing mostly training exercises during her career. She served the Royal Canadian Navy the longest of all the Bay of Quinte ships, with 10 years of continuous service. Unlike the other ships, she served in a time of peace. This does not diminish her role or importance to the Quinte area or the navy.

This statement written for *Quinte* on her paying off most respectfully summarizes the ship and her influence of the Royal Canadian Navy: "No one can say what the future holds for her, but the achievements of her past will not be soon forgotten, for there were many who received their first knowledge of the ways of the sea on her decks."[47]

Her bell is proudly displayed at the 8 Wing/Canadian Forces Base Trenton Yacht Club, located on the Bay of Quinte.

AWARDS EARNED BY CREW

- Orville Earl Guest, Petty Officer Second Class (PO2), RCN: Queen's Commendation for Brave Conduct

  Petty Officer Guest was instrumental in saving the life of a member of the gate vessel HMCS PORTE SAINT-JEAN, who fell overboard and struck his head on the side of the jetty. Petty Officer Guest held the man's head above water and at the same time, fended the gate vessel off the jetty with his body, until both were hauled up to safety. There is no doubt that had not Petty Officer Guest taken this timely action in this dangerous situation, the Able Seaman would have drowned.

DND UB347. Photo courtesy Archives and Collections Society, Picton.

The official badge of HMCS Quinte. *RCSCC Quinte in Belleville, Ontario, has the badge on display at the Sea Cadet building.*

Commanding Officers

D.P. Brownlow, LCDR, RCN	15 October 1954 to 23 June 1957
R.P. Mylea, LCDR, RCN	24 June 1957 to 2 September 1959
R.J. Paul, LCDR, RCN	3 September 1959 to 2 August 1961
G.G. Armstrong, LCDR, RCN	3 August 1961 to 30 July 1963
R.L. Donaldson, LCDR, RCN	31 July 1963 to 26 February 1964

**HMCS *QUINTE*
BATTLE HONOURS**

ATLANTIC   1941–1942

Specifications

Name:	HMCS *Quinte* (II), named for Bay of Quinte		
Classification:	Bay-class minesweeper		
Builder:	Port Arthur Shipbuilding Company Limited — Port Arthur, Ontario		
Keel Laid: 14/06/52	Launched: 08/08/53	Commissioned: 15/10/54	Paid Off: 26/02/64
Length: 152 feet	Beam: 28 feet	Draught: 8 feet	
Displacement: 390 tons	Speed: 16 knots	Fuel: not available	
Crew: 3 officers, 35 other ranks		Machinery: Diesel engine	
Armament:	one single 40 mm machine gun, minesweeping gear		

Specifications of HMCS Quinte.

Chart prepared by Roger Litwiller.

CHAPTER 7

HMCS *TRENTONIAN*
K368
REVISED FLOWER-CLASS
CORVETTE
INCREASED ENDURANCE
1942–1943 PROGRAM

Photo courtesy Gary McGregor.

HMCS Trentonian *in Montreal, December 1943.*

IN NOVEMBER 1942, THE CITY OF Trenton, Ontario, sent a letter to Naval Service Head Quarters (NSHQ) in Ottawa. The letter expressed the community's wishes to have a ship named after the city. The name Trenton was rejected by NSHQ because of the American cruiser USS *Trenton*, as they didn't want to duplicate the names of ships in Allied navies. So a list of alternative names was given: Trentonia, Trent, Quinte, and Mount Pelion. Two of the names were already in use as *HMCS Quinte* and HMS *Trent*.

Naval Service Headquarters chose *Trentonia* and added it to the list of new ships for construction. When the clerk was typing the list, *Trentonia* followed the name of another ship, *Prestonian*, and an "N" was accidentally added on the end of her name. The list with *Trentonian* was sent to the king and received royal approval.

The error was not caught until after the name had received royal consent and therefore could not be changed. Historically, sailors are a superstitious lot with some unique beliefs and practices: it is "bad luck" to sail on a Friday, no women or cats aboard a ship, and whistling will bring a storm. Another major superstitious belief is that to change the name of a ship is to seal its fate in disaster, and thus the ship received her name and the city received her ship.

HMCS *Trentonian* was built at Kingston Shipyards, with her keel laid on 19 February 1943 as hull number 27.[1] The citizens of Trenton took an active role in her construction and made frequent trips to Kingston to watch her progress. Additionally, a committee was formed in the city with many prominent residents taking an active role in planning and preparing to support their ship. Her launching and christening ceremony was attended by a large group

Crowds gather at the Kingston Shipyard as Trentonian *is ready for launching on 1 September 1943.*

of Trentonians representing the City of Trenton, and the wine bottle was broken across her bow by Mrs. Cory, the wife of the mayor.

HMCS *Trentonian* was commissioned into the Royal Canadian Navy on 1 December 1943, under the command of Lieutenant William Edward Harrison, RCNR, from Lunenburg, Nova Scotia. Harrison was described by his men as a strong skipper, always concerned about his ship and his crew. On taking command of *Trentonian*, he was already a veteran of the Battle of Atlantic with 30 months sea time. He had commanded two ships prior to *Trentonian*: the armed yacht, HMCS *Husky*, and another corvette HMCS *Lunenburg*.

On 3 December 1943, *Trentonian* departed the Great Lakes not yet complete so as not to be frozen in for the winter. She arrived in Montreal on 6 December for a three-day layover and then proceeded to Quebec City, arriving on 10 December.

While in Quebec City, the majority of her new crew reported aboard. The weather was clear and bitterly cold; the crew quarters in the messdecks were freezing. As the temperature outside dropped, so did the temperature inside the ship, despite the new insulation that had been installed to keep the ship warm. When ice began to form above them on the deckhead, the men threatened to walk off the ship. Engineers were called in to examine the problem and found

Photo courtesy Bruce Keir.

Trentonian *at Halifax with a new coat of paint in March 1944.*

that the exhaust fans had been installed backwards and were blowing the cold air into the ship instead of ventilating the air out. The problem was remedied, and the crew settled in for their first warm night. With time *Trentonian* became known as a "happy ship."[2]

Lieutenant Harrison wrote his first letter to Trenton on 17 December 1943, addressed to Hazel Farley, the local liaison with the ship. Miss Farley was a teacher at Trenton High School and coordinated all communication with the ship and crew on behalf of the committee. She also started a pen-pal program between the students and the crew.

In war, censorship was always necessary, and Harrison could not always write about what was truly happening with his ship, nor could he give her location. With this in mind, his first letter reads as follows:

HMCS TRENTONIAN
c/o FMO Halifax
17 Dec 1943

Dear Miss Farley

Your letter and parcel with afghans arrived yesterday. Many thanks for both. Some of the men have, I hear, already received letters from their pen-pals. They appear to be delighted with them so I hope the friendship by correspondence lasts. Sailors are notoriously bad correspondents but some of them make up for the others.

You asked about quilts. I'm sure they would be useful, but a limited amount as there are only nine bunks in the ship. As for your other questions socks and mitts are always acceptable, little pictures that they can stick up to improve the scenery and a very urgent need at the moment — ashtrays. However we don't really want to trespass on your generosity except for the little things that perhaps would be easily got hold of.

Things are still hectic here, still wet paint around and ends of wires. We have also got the dismal news that we will spend Xmas at sea so that won't be so hot in more senses than one. It couldn't be much colder than it is here at any rate. However, we will have quite a time finishing off when we get there so the above address should find us for a few more weeks.

I am still living on shore not having my cabin finished yet. They have decided to run a lot more wires and a ventilating shaft right through it.

Well, I fancy I have to go out in the cold again so won't put it off any longer.

Yours Sincerely
WE Harrison[3]

Trentonian received her orders to slip her lines and proceed to Halifax on 23 December 1943, but due to weather and ice conditions her sailing was delayed until the 26th. This gave the ship and her crew their first Christmas together alongside the docks at Quebec City. Christmas was celebrated in the usual customs of the Navy, with the youngest member of the crew assuming the role of skipper for the day.

Trentonian departed Quebec for Halifax and arrived on 29 December, when the remainder of her crew joined the ship. The crew of *Trentonian* was very diverse, the same as all warships that have ever been in commission in the Canadian Navy. They represent all of Canada in one tight little community. There are the coasters, coming from the East and West Coasts, the Prairie boys, Quebecers, and those from central Canada. In *Trentonian's* crew every major Canadian city was represented as well as many small towns.

Following a two-day layover in Halifax, she was sent to Liverpool, Nova Scotia, for her final fitting out, arriving on New Year's Eve, 1943, where she would remain for a month.

On return to Halifax, *Trentonian* was sent to Bermuda for training evolutions and workups, leaving on 18 February 1944. The trip to Bermuda found *Trentonian* in a proper North Atlantic winter storm. She was in seas estimated to be 90 feet in height. The majority of the crew was disabled with seasickness and given a forty-eight-hour stand down to recover from the ordeal.

While docking in Bermuda, *Trentonian* received minor damage to a ventilator and hatch when the engine telegraph stuck in the full-ahead position, causing a forward berthing line to draw taught and snap. This damage caused a leak into the forward messdeck that, despite several attempts, was never fixed.

Photo courtesy Quinte West Public Library.

Crew photo taken in Halifax during a snowstorm in January 1944.

Unlike her sister ships constructed earlier in the war, which sailed directly to conflict upon completion, *Trentonian* and her crew were given the opportunity to train for war. Acting Captain J.D. Prentice and Acting Commander J. Waterhouse oversaw the working up of the ship and the exercising of the crew in all their duties and responsibilities.[4]

Trentonian*'s bridge is full of activity during training evolutions in Bermuda in February 1944.*

Over the course of nine days, the crew was steadily involved in gunnery and anti-submarine exercises, damage control, abandon ship drills, inspections, and so forth. During one of the gunnery evolutions for the anti-aircraft guns, the gun's crew began to celebrate, as they felt extremely confident they had "blown away" the target towed behind the aircraft. The conducting officer then ordered the aircraft to fly past the ship, and to the dismay of the gun's crew the target was untouched. With practice, they later not only hit the target, but blew away the cable attaching the target to the airplane.[5]

Nine days is not enough time for the officers and men to fully learn a new ship, let alone to prepare for live combat aboard her, but this was standard for

While in Bermuda, the entire crew train and learn to operate the ship as a team.

the time and actually an improvement from a year before. When Commander Waterhouse summed up the report for *Trentonian*, he praised the young crew for trying their best with a ship that was new and still not fully finished. He commented about the lack of sea time and therefore inexperience of the junior officers, but added that they showed an eagerness to learn. He concluded his report with the following general impression: "Ships are always a little worse than their officers. If the officers do not know what various

Trentonian *returns to Halifax from Bermuda, covered in ice from a North Atlantic storm in March 1944.*

articles are for or in what condition various fittings are in, the crew will take even less interest and deterioration will be rapid. The officers of this ship must get to work and learn their ship and having learned it must inspect it frequently until it is up to standard."[6]

The return from Bermuda again had *Trentonian* facing another North Atlantic winter storm. This one wasn't as severe as during the trip down, but the ship received damage to her water tanks, necessitating repairs at Halifax.

A merchant ship from Trentonian's *first convoy, HX 283, bound for Liverpool from Halifax on 19 March 1944.*

Trentonian went on active service, escorting convoys from Canada's East Coast. She was ordered to join her first convoy on 15 March with *New Glasgow*, *Louisburg* (II), and *Drumheller*. Convoy HX 283 had departed from New York City on 13 March, en route to Liverpool, and consisted of 62 ships. The convoy proceeded without incident. On 19 March, *Trentonian*, along with *New Glasgow*, *Louisburg* (II), *Drumheller*, and HMCS *Stormont*, were diverted away from the convoy to search for a suspected nearby German submarine, without success.

One submarine *Trentonian* did find was the Royal Navy submarine *P-223*, which was damaged by ice and unable to dive. The German submarine threat was so great that the Allies issued a very simple order concerning all contacts with submarines: "Sink all submarines on sight." This placed the RN submarine in a very dangerous position, and on 3 April 1944 *Trentonian* was detailed to find and escort her to the Royal Navy base at Argentia, Newfoundland. Technology then was not as it is today, and the submarine and *Trentonian* were unable to communicate directly with each other. Both ships would radio their position to command in Newfoundland and then work toward each other, a slow method of communication that relies heavily on the navigation skill of the individual crews.

Trentonian did not spot the surfaced submarine until late in the day on 4 April. On sighting the submarine, *Trentonian's* crew was immediately closed up to action stations and all guns were trained on the submarine, with the anti-submarine weapons placed at the ready. Tensions remained high until the two small ships were able to close the distance to each other and make a positive identification.[7] They both arrived safely in Argentia the next day.

On arrival at Halifax, *Trentonian* was again placed in the hands of the dock workers and had new radar and four additional machine guns installed, two in the waist and two aft of the after gun tub. Unknown to the crew, she would need the additional anti-aircraft guns for her future work in British waters. Of course, this also required the crew to paint the ship after the dock workers were finished.

On 23 April 1944, she left Halifax for England with her sister ships *Lindsay* and *Louisburg* (II). During the transit, the small fleet was diverted twice, first on

Photo courtesy Bruce Keir.

Trentonian rescues this damaged Royal Navy submarine, P225, and escorts her to Newfoundland in April 1944.

25 April to search for a suspected German submarine believed to be patrolling near the route of the three ships. After several hours of asdic sweeps with no contact, the search was called off. The second diversion was on 27 April to search for survivors of a merchant ship lost in the area, but the search was called off later that day as they had been found by another ship. The remainder of the time was spent on normal operations and exercising the ship and the crew. Since it was still early in the year, icebergs were found along their route and each posed an opportunity for the gun crews to use it for target practice.

Of course, judging fall of shot and accuracy was very difficult as the icebergs exploded with white ice.[8] All three ships arrived in Londonderry a week later on 1 May 1944.[9]

Upon arrival, *Trentonian* was immediately assigned to training, evolutions, and workups for two weeks. The crew attended combat school during the day, learning how to work the ship and use her equipment in all kinds of scenarios. When the classroom portion was over, the crew took *Trentonian* out for live practice with the ship. During one of these evolutions, the gun crew was training with the anti-aircraft

Photo courtesy Bruce Keir.

The crew of Trentonian *learn the reality of war when they spot this freighter, believed to be* SS Moderita, *in St. John's Harbour, Newfoundland.*

Photo courtesy Tom Farrell.

On arrival in Londonderry in May 1944, the crew takes every opportunity to train, including gunnery drills in harbour.

guns on a towed aircraft. High importance was given to anti-aircraft gunnery, as the German Luftwaffe was a constant threat to all shipping. When the exercise was over, the entire crew was called up on deck and two Spitfires flew close down each side of the ship, strafing the water right alongside, sending up geysers of water. This was to give the crew an idea of what a real air attack would be like.[10]

The crew of *Trentonian* had been training to play an active role in the imminent invasion of France. The naval portion of the invasion was called

Operation Neptune, and the army portion was Operation Overlord. Today we know the entire invasion as D-Day.

On 23 May 1944, *Trentonian* departed for Oban, Scotland.[11] She was assigned the position of senior officer of the first convoy to leave for the beaches of Normandy. Together with *Mayflower*, *Drumheller*, *Rimouski*, *Louisburg*, and HMS *Nasturtium*, she left on 31 May 1944 with a convoy of derelict ships.[12] These ships were destined to be sunk off the beachhead to form the breakwater of the artificial harbour that was to be constructed at the invasion site.

While at sea, Harrison informed the crew of the upcoming invasion and the part *Trentonian* was about to play. Some of the crew took to writing letters home and reflecting with their messmates. One in particular, a 22-year-old signalman, decided to start a journal; his first entry reads as follows:

> The Old Man called the crew together for a "pep talk" on what is about to happen. I am going to have a ringside seat to the biggest thing in warfare that man has ever conceived or attempted. We are now in the English Channel, shepherding our convoy like a big wandering flock of sheep under the watchful eye of British fighter and bomber

Photo courtesy Bruce Keir.

Trentonian *arrives off the Normandy beachhead for the invasion of France.*

aircraft. This strip of water, will in a day or two without a doubt become the hottest spot on earth. And I shall be at the very vortex of this man-made hell! In case I do not survive perhaps someday someone will say, "He died doing his duty!" It has been estimated that 85% of the men taking part in this invasion will not come out of it. Well everyone is hoping that he will be one of the 15% left but also resolved to go down fighting if he is not.[13]

Trentonian arrived off the beaches of Normandy in the early morning hours of 7 June 1944 and spent the next several days on continuous duty, escorting a variety of convoys from England to France.[14] *Trentonian* was the only one of the Bay of Quinte ships to play an active role in Operation Neptune.

Following the invasion, *Trentonian* was assigned to a highly secretive escort duty. As part of the PLUTO (Pipe Line Under the Ocean) program, the mission and the ships involved were highly classified. Part of the program was to lay an underwater fuel pipeline from England to France so the army would have a safe supply of fuel to move forward. The other part was to

This troop ship took up station near Trentonian, *and, as the Canadian soldiers were taken ashore, they spotted the maple leaf on* Trentonian's *funnel and cheered.*

lay an underwater communications cable from command in England to the front lines in France, in order to allow secure and uninterrupted communications.

Just after 0300 on the morning of 12 June 1944, *Trentonian* rendezvoused with the two British cable ships, HMTS *Monarch* and HMTS *St. Margaret*, and the cable barge *Norman*, off The Needles in the English Channel. From there she escorted them toward the coast of Normandy, *St. Margaret* laying her cable first. The cable ships travelled at a slow speed as they worked, so *Trentonian* escorted them closely in a circular pattern at about 500 to 700 yards distance.[15]

One of *Trentonian's* crew wrote in his journal, "dull and tedious job, spinning circles around this small collection of ships," while other ratings remarked this was not a job for a fighting ship, especially with all the action around them. The invasion was in full swing, important troop and cargo convoys were everywhere, and the other escorts were right in the thick of it.[16]

The bellyaching and griping of the crew passed right by *Trentonian's* skipper; in fact, he welcomed it. Just before D-Day, Lieutenant Harrison sent a thank you letter to the city of Trenton. When he mentioned the crew and their performance, he was very pleased that the crew had built quite a respectable reputation

Photo courtesy Bruce Keir.

Two landing ships race past Trentonian *to the beach.*

for themselves and the ship. He also went on to state, "They have lots to grumble about so are perfectly happy. A good old growl is a great pastime and gives them something in common." Knowing just what the possible future could hold for his ship and crew, Harrison finished the letter, "Well, I hope we still stick together. I'd like to bring everybody back to Canada that left with us and I am sure we will manage that."[17]

Over the next 10 hours, St. Margaret and Norman laid out the communications cable onto the floor of the channel. When their cable had been extended, the task of joining the cable to Monarch began. This took an additional seven hours, the two ships and barge holding position and Trentonian still turning circles around them.

The tedium was finally broken at 1340, when word passed through the ship that three aircraft had been spotted nearby, circling a group of passing Landing Craft (LSTs) en route to Normandy. The crew filtered on deck to watch, when bombs started to drop around the LSTs, sending up great geysers of water. Luftwaffe activity had been pretty scarce over the channel in the past few days, and only when they made the attack were they identified as German. The bombs missed their targets, and a dozen Spitfires appeared and immediately dealt with the three German planes.[18]

At 1600 St. Margaret and Norman were sent back to Portsmouth under the escort of the British corvette HMS Dianthus. This left Trentonian with Monarch, who was still motionless at this point, for the final phase of the cable lay to France.[19]

Shortly after, at 1645, Trentonian's crew was called to action stations. A hydrophone effect was heard, sounding like a torpedo, and a strong asdic contact was made. She increased speed to 16 knots and patrolled a line between Monarch and the contact,

then dropped three depth charges set shallow with no positive effect. The asdic contact slowly decreased and was finally lost.

Monarch finally began to move again at 2000, slowly making her way toward the beaches, laying out the cable. The sky was now dark and heavy anti-aircraft fire, tracer fire, and starshell could be seen in all directions at varying distances.

At midnight, as the day changed to 13 June, Trentonian reported, "Picked up contact on starboard side, probably E-Boat. This contact was immediately engaged by four escort vessels that were passing, bound north, and was not heard again. Carrying out circular screen around Monarch, distant 500–700 yards, speed 11 knots. Starshell and tracer being fired all around the horizon."[20]

Tensions were growing in Trentonian; since this escort job had started almost 21 hours before, they made contact with the enemy in the air, on the water, and possibly beneath it. The only contact not yet made was with shore batteries, and that possibility was growing as the two ships approached the occupied coast of France. Harrison ordered extra lookouts to be posted around the ship.

The two ships were alone in the darkness, but hundreds of Allied ships surrounded them as an American destroyer group was on patrol nearby. At 0100 the closest destroyer to Trentonian, USS Plunkett, noted in their log, "At this time a good deal of activity was apparent to the northward and many starshell were observed in this area throughout the earlier part of the night. At about this time two targets were picked up bearing about north. Conversation on the TBS and TBL (radio) intercepted prior to this had led me to expect the appearance of our own forces in this sector and these targets were assumed to be friendly."[21]

An hour later *Plunkett* heard a query by USS *Davis*, the destroyer next in line to her, raising some questions about the two radar contacts they had assumed to be friendly. A reply was given to the question but the message itself was not heard in *Plunkett*. This raised doubts for her commanding officer and with the range between the two groups at 9,000 yards, time for answers was shrinking.

Thirty minutes later, at 0230, the tedium began to unravel and was being replaced by confusion. *Plunkett* ordered starshell to be fired over the two radar contacts now only 4,500 yards distant. She reported that the starshell failed to work properly due to the close range. While *Trentonian* noted that starshell illuminated the sky above her and the cable ship, initially her crew could not see the direction the starshell had been fired from. The two ships were now well within range of the German occupied coast. One of the lookouts reported several destroyers visible on either bow, approaching from some distance.

Two minutes later *Plunkett* again fired starshell, and this time due to an error the shells struck the water before illuminating. With the range between the ships rapidly closing, *Plunkett* made another attempt to contact the two ships, this time flashing the minor warship challenge at the nearest ship, *Monarch*.

At this point confusion gave way to chaos. It is not known if *Monarch* received this signal. *Monarch* was under the command of Captain Eric Troops, a retired Royal Navy officer who had served in cable ships for many years. Unknown to the American destroyer, *Monarch*'s orders were to follow a lighted signal from shore and not respond to it. *Plunkett* was now in the same location as the expected signal from shore; the signal was repeated three times, ten seconds apart, and after one minute with no response from the ship being challenged, *Plunkett* opened fire at 3,000 yards.[22]

Harrison in *Trentonian* noted at 0235, "Firing commenced on a bearing of 160 degrees. No gun flashes were seen. Shells were heard, apparently close, afterwards passing between the two ships, then coming directly towards *Trentonian*. All shots fired at or near *Trentonian* were high, except two or three which struck the water ahead and one which passed between the funnel and the pom-pom platform." Fortunately for *Trentonian* and her crew, all the incoming rounds missed the ship.

Harrison ordered the recognition lights to be flashed on and off. Aboard *Trentonian* it seemed as if the fire was then redirected solely at *Monarch*. As the shells started to smash into the cable ship, the sounds were overwhelming. The barrage balloon above her came crashing down on her decks, and the whine of the shells was overpowered by the constant piercing shrill of *Monarch*'s steam whistle.

Harrison ordered *Trentonian* turned broadside to the attacking ship in hopes of a friendly identification being made and to stop the incoming fire. The assault on *Monarch* then appeared to switch back to *Trentonian*.

Again the shells missed, spraying *Trentonian* with geysers of water. Harrison ordered every light in the ship turned on and placed *Trentonian* between the two ships; the range had now closed to 600 yards.

As soon as the recognition lights were observed, *Plunkett* ceased fire. The total time of the attack was less than five minutes, and it is estimated that 80 rounds of five-inch ammunition was expended by *Plunkett*. *Monarch* bore the brunt of the attack; *Trentonian* was undamaged.

Photo courtesy Bruce Keir.

The cable-laying ship, HMTS Monarch *showing the severe damage after the accidental attack by an American destroyer.*

The three ships were joined by a second American destroyer, USS *Davis*. All four ships came to anchor around the damaged *Monarch*, and *Plunkett* and *Davis* immediately sent their doctors over to the cable ship to render aid. *Trentonian* sent over a damage control party to *Monarch* and picked up some of her crew that had been thrown into the water by the explosions. They were taken into *Trentonian* and given medical care.

Plunkett sent a boat with a junior officer to *Trentonian*. When he came aboard, he apologized for his commanding officer, stating that he was a

bit trigger-happy, and explained they had mistaken the two ships for German torpedo boats. The bridge crew reported that Harrison did not say a word and instead he let his executive officer, Lieutenant Kinsmen, speak to the young ensign. Harrison could only glare at the young American officer with silent rage. After the Americans had left, the crew said he was fit to be tied, demanding a court martial: "How could they mistake us for E-boats — we are three to four times their size."

As the sun rose, the damage to *Monarch* became evident: her superstructure was badly damaged and

Photo courtesy Bruce Keir.

A closer view of the shell damage to Monarch *that killed and wounded several of her crew.*

her bridge was blown away, her compass was smashed, and the steering gear was beyond repair. The communications cable, so vital to the war effort, was gone, severed and lying somewhere at the bottom of the channel. The chief officer and a seaman, both on the bridge, had been killed. Her skipper, Captain Troops, had a severe head injury and was in critical condition. Four others were critically wounded; many more were wounded to a lesser degree.

The most severe of the wounded, after receiving care from the American doctors, were transferred into *Trentonian*. Captain Troops was not expected to live.

The two American destroyers then resumed their patrol. *Trentonian* started back to England, leading *Monarch* without compass and steering by hand. She eventually made England, where she was taken in tow by tugs, and *Trentonian* arrived in Portsmouth, where ambulances were waiting on the jetty. As feared, Captain Troops died of his wounds before reaching harbour, in Harrison's cabin.[23]

After the wounded had landed, *Trentonian* was sent to anchor in a distant section of the harbour and the crew denied shore leave. In short order, some of the Navy's brass had come aboard and the crew

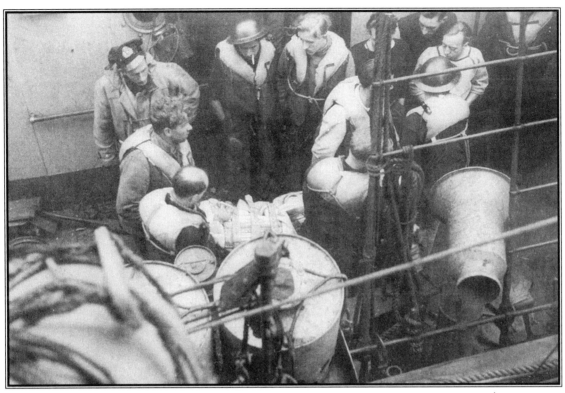

Photo courtesy Bruce Kerr.

Critically wounded crew members of Monarch *are moved to* Trentonian.

was told in no uncertain terms not to discuss this incident with anyone and to keep their mouths shut. There was no sense putting unnecessary strain on inter-Allied relations. With this, the secret had been kept. This incident was not made public in any detail until 1953.[24]

Trentonian and her crew were kept on active duty, escorting convoys almost continuously following the invasion, and she escorted 12 convoys from various locations around England to the beachhead during this time. It was not until 5 July 1944 that the crew was able to stand down from duties and take a much needed rest, while their ship received a boiler cleaning and underwent a maintenance period. Lieutenant

Harrison took the opportunity to write another letter to the city of Trenton; he summarizes the work of the ship and the condition of the crew during the past several weeks of strenuous operations:

HMCS *Trentonian*
c/o GPO London
July 11th 1944

Dear Miss Farley

Thanks for your letter of the 1st of June which I just received. Also a parcel of records arrived today in very good condition. We have now got a gramophone or rather a radiogram which is connected up with five loud speakers in different parts of the ship, so everyone gets the benefit of either broadcast or records. So far we have had rather a scarcity of records and the same thing came over and over again, but now we shall have lots of variety. I must congratulate whoever chose the records. I have just been looking through them and all the sailors favorites are there. I can hear "Waltzing Matilda" now as I write. This evening we will broadcast them through the loudspeaker on the mast so the ships alongside will get the benefit. The Victrola has not yet turned up but it will probably arrive sometime.

We have just had a short spell in port and all the crew had two days leave which the majority chose to spend dodging "buzz bombs" in London. Previous to that nobody had been off the ship for 42 days, since 22nd of May, so the break did a lot of good.

As you probably know, we took part in the invasion of Normandy and although it wasn't as exciting as we expected it to be, there was great deal of hard work attached to it and to subsequent operations which are not of course yet finished. The censors have very kindly told us that we can divulge the fact of being connected with the invasion and I think full advantage has been taken of the lifting of this restriction, so you have probably heard some highly coloured tales which would perhaps conflict with our rather monotonous recollections.

Our mail is still very scrappy some letters come in a couple of weeks and others take five or six weeks. However, I suppose we're lucky to be getting so much. When the North African business was taking place, we didn't get any mail in the Mediterranean for about three months. This has been a big improvement.

Please tell the Grade X pupils how much we appreciate the records. They are really very popular already although they haven't all been tried yet. Thanking you all.

I remain
Yours very sincerely
W.E. Harrison[25]

Following the invasion, *Trentonian* continued to work the English Channel and the Bay of Biscay, escorting convoys around England to France and performing anti-submarine sweeps. The crew had been given the opportunity for a brief shore leave in Cherbourg, France, shortly after the port city had been liberated by the Allies. The crew was instructed to travel in only large groups at all times. The reason given: German soldiers were still being captured inside the city.[26]

Early in the morning of 11 September 1944, *Trentonian* once again departed England, this time escorting convoy EBC 100 from the Bristol Channel to France.[27] The next day, when the convoy was in the Irish Sea, *Trentonian* came across two large oil barges adrift, and she detached from the convoy to take the barges in tow. The task of recovering the barges took several hours of very difficult manoeuvring, requiring the ship to come to a full stop while the barges were secured. This allowed *Trentonian* to drift with the tide and current, and unfortunately this brought the ship into the middle of a minefield. The crew reported mines on either side of their ship, and sharp-shooters were brought up on deck. By this time the mines were so close that to intentionally detonate them could destroy the ship. The men watched from the rails with bated breath as Harrison slowly manoeuvred *Trentonian*, with the barges in tow, successfully through the minefield and into the safety of the channel.[28]

Photo courtesy Tom Ferrill.

Trentonian takes in tow two fuel barges adrift in a mine-field. The crew watched as mines drifted a short distance from *Trentonian's* side.

The following month, *Trentonian* departed Milford Haven on 15 October escorting a large, floating concrete block towed by two tugs, *Saucy* and *Hesperia*. The concrete block was part of a prefabricated dock and would be sunk off France, allowing merchant ships to discharge their cargo directly to shore. A concrete block does not handle with the grace of a ship and so was very difficult to control. The handling of this tow was made all the more difficult as the weather was deteriorating, with the wind increasing and the sea state at force 9-10.

Finally, after two days of fighting the sea and wind, the towline snapped from the tug *Hesperia*. Over the next two hours, with great physical hardship, the five-man crew on the block attempted to attach a new towline to the tug *Saucy*. Before a second attempt was made, the crew was given a chance to rest, and finally a line was attached from *Saucy* to the block at 1830 after a six-hour struggle. Unfortunately, the weather had continued to deteriorate and *Saucy* did not have the power to tow the massive concrete block against the now gale-force winds. She sent a message to *Trentonian* that she would hold in position.

The new towline broke just one hour after it was secure, and the crews attempted to secure another. Finally, after two hours and with darkness approaching, the five men on the block were removed and it was allowed to drift for the night. *Trentonian* and the two tugs remained close by, as the block was not fitted with lights and was an extreme collision hazard to other ships.

The next morning, the weather was beginning to co-operate as the wind and sea started to die down, but it was not until afternoon that a crew could be put back aboard the concrete block safely. It was almost 1500 when a line was secured and the block was once again in tow and proceeding toward France.

Three hours later, fate would intervene once more as the cement block took a sudden list of about

Photo courtesy Bruce Keir.

Trentonian's boat crew rescues the men trapped on board this sinking portion of the artificial harbour used at Normandy.

15 degrees, and the crew on the block reported it was taking water through a six-foot hole in its side and was now in danger of sinking. A Royal Navy minesweeper that had joined the little fleet earlier, HMS *Inverforth*, managed to position herself alongside the block and take aboard eight of its 10 men before becoming entangled in the towlines. If the massive block sank, now she could drag the minesweeper down with her. *Inverforth* cleared the lines as quickly as she could and moved away from the block, and *Trentonian* then sent her whaler in to rescue the last two men remaining on the block.

The cement block continued to fill with water, and at 2020 *Trentonian* was ordered to proceed toward Barry Roads, leaving the tugs to wait for the block's eventual end. The tug *Saucy* reported by radio that the cement block finally sank 45 minutes later.[29]

From D-Day in June until November 1944, *Trentonian* escorted over 45 convoys around England to France. Lieutenant Harrison took advantage of an extended boiler cleaning to update the city of Trenton:

HMCS *Trentonian*
11 November 1944

Dear Miss Farley

Thank you for your letter of Oct. 18th also card which arrived the same time. I'm glad that you got the photographs alright.

We are having a fairly agreeable time over here, the weather is a bit miserable at times but we can't complain. The chief question now is, "How much longer," of course, but there is not much indication of us returning in the near future.

Your list of things which are on our way to us sounds very generous indeed. You and your friends are spoiling us all.

As far as magazines are concerned the favorites are still such as "American Colliers," "Red Book," "Saturday Evening Post" and as there are five messes, five copies would be greatly appreciated. Half the ship's company have had seven days leave recently and have spent it in different parts of this country. They are getting to know their way around now, and, I think, feel quite at home in Britain.

We have had the good fortune to spend a couple of weeks recently at a large seaport town where they all had a very good time.

Our regular base is only a small place and I think they have got a bit fed up with it. There are several other Canadian Corvettes with us and they see their friends on the other ships pretty frequently so that's quite a break.

Here's hoping you all enjoy a Very Happy Xmas and a good holiday at the end of the year.

Best wishes to all your "Flock"
Sincerely
W.E. Harrison[30]

Photo courtesy Tom Ferrell.

After many months of continuous convoy escort, HMCS Trentonian *is given a new coat of paint and a new camouflage pattern, in October 1944.*

Trentonian continued with her hectic schedule of escorting convoys through November and December, fighting several storms during these winter months. She arrived at Milford Haven, her primary base of operations during the early morning hours on Christmas Eve 1944. She was to have a day of rest and had received orders to sail again in the late afternoon of Christmas Day. Harrison was adamant that his men were going to enjoy Christmas dinner in port, and informed the senior officer that his ship could not sail until later, hoping to have the orders changed to 26 December

The crew of *Trentonian* enjoyed a marvelous feast of turkey, dressing, and all the trimmings, prepared by her cooks. They reflected on how far they had come and some of the "sticky" messes they had found themselves in. Also the big question, "When will it be over?" Supper was no sooner finished and the men about to take a moment to relax when Harrison received his orders to slip and proceed to sea immediately. He was frustrated by the fact that so many ships were in harbour before *Trentonian* had arrived and were still there now, while his ship was ordered out ahead of these others. He cleared lower decks, calling "hands to stations for leaving harbour." Once clear of the dock, he ordered "full speed ahead," sending out a huge wake, knocking the sleeping ships about.[31]

They would spend New Year's at sea, escorting two convoys before returning to Milford Haven on 2 January 1945. *Trentonian* was due for another boiler cleaning, and Harrison used the time to update the city of Trenton with another letter:

6th January 1945

Dear Miss Farley

Have just received a very large batch of letters and parcels. All kinds of gifts from Trenton included. There are a lot of things which you mention sending which haven't arrived yet but doubtless will turn up in time. I will give you a list now of what we actually have received from all sources in Trenton. A very imposing list too -80 wallets -80 boxes of chocolates -32,000 cigarettes -75 woolen socks, 15 mitts — Gramophone records — Washing machine — Writing kits. (I think there were 80 writing kits but as half the ship's company are on leave I can't check on it at the moment — all the people who handled the distribution are away.)

You can see that several shipments which you mention have not arrived yet (plum puddings, etc.). I also have a letter from Mrs. C.V. Wilkins telling me of a shipment of socks by the Red Cross. These are not turned up yet but I will let her know when they do. The washing machine arrived before Xmas and is now operating very successfully. By the way the Victrola that you sent the same time as the records is not here yet. I mailed a list of the ship's company to you the other day so you should have it soon. Our numbers alternate around 104 men all told. There is a little variation sometimes we get down to a hundred when a couple go to hospital or are absent for some reason.

We distributed the personal gifts as follows. The 80 wallets arrived first and went to the 80 who had been in the ship the longest — the ones left out got a box of chocolates. The writing kits were drawn for, the losers getting chocolates again. The remaining chocolates were distributed to the messes. I think everybody appreciated the gifts as I'm sure they should, there being very few

Canadian ships as well and as consistently looked after as well as we are. Some of the bigger cities which have adopted ships started off with a very expensive splash, but so far as I hear their enthusiasm died down after a few months.

I'm sure you are very much responsible for the fact that we have not been forgotten for a moment even though we are so far away and the difficulty of shipping things so great. As I was writing the last sentence a large parcel has arrived addressed to me. I see it is marked "Knit goods" and has Mrs. Whitley's name on the label. I have had it locked away not to be opened until we get out of dock, as the ship is teeming with acquisitive workmen and the men don't need them till we leave.

Hoping that you are enjoying 1945 and wishing you all the best in the coming year.

Yours Sincerely
W.E. Harrison[32]

On 21 January 1945, Lieutenant Harrison received a message that brought mixed feelings for him; he was promoted to acting lieutenant commander. Although all good naval officers are looking to better themselves, the recognition of his service came with a cost: he was to take command of a larger ship, HMCS *Joliette*. His new command was a River-class frigate commissioned only six months before. With this in mind, Lieutenant Commander Harrison wrote his final letter to the citizens of Trenton:

25th January 1945

Miss Hazel Farley

It is with a certain amount of sadness that I write to you this time, because it is to inform you that I am leaving the old ship in a couple of days. I have been appointed to a frigate, HMCS *Joliette*, and will be joining her shortly.

Almost as much as I regret leaving the ship and her happy and efficient ship's company, I regret breaking my official connection with yourself, and the many good folks of Trenton who have interested themselves in the ship. It has been a very pleasant experience for me to have been connected with you all.

I hope that one of these days we shall all meet again. Who knows?

The new Commanding Officer will be Lieut. C. Glassco RCNVR and I will pass on to him all my records of things that have been done or undone i.e. the balance between what has been sent and what has been received. There are one or two things still in the mail, as I mentioned in my last letter.

Please say Goodbye, for me, to all the girls and boys, and give them my very best wishes and my thanks for their good work and self-sacrifice on our behalf.

Tell them all, teachers and pupils, that if I ever get another chance to visit them, they won't terrify me quite so much the second time. (I believe everyone in Joliette speaks French, so pity me if I ever go <u>there</u>.)

Well I'll say Au Revoir (just to get in practice) to all of you and would like you to know that I shall always remember you and my visit to you, with pleasure.

My sincere good wishes,
W.E. Harrison[33]

Command of *Trentonian* was passed to Lieutenant Colin S. Glassco, RCNVR, of Hamilton on 31 January 1945. The new skipper was met with some trepidation; he was untested and strict, something the crew did not appreciate this late in the war. They had followed Harrison from the day *Trentonian* was commissioned and he had kept them safe and out of harm's way.

Lieutenant Glassco had just come from the corvette HMCS *Ville de Quebec*, where he was her executive officer. Prior to this, he had been the commanding officer of several naval reserve divisions in Canada. *Trentonian* was his first command of a warship.[34] Glassco commented years later in an interview with the Trenton newspaper about his new command, "I was lucky in succeeding Lieutenant Harrison, an excellent officer and so I inherited a well-trained crew and a group of excellent officers."[35] This showed a marked improvement in the comments from *Trentonian*'s workups in Bermuda, which cited a lack of experience, and gives great credit to the officers and crew.

Glassco's first order was very unpopular: no one was to be on the outer decks without a lifejacket on

at any time. This made work on the outer decks difficult, as the new RCN lifejackets were cumbersome. But the crew knew *Trentonian* was due for a refit; the paperwork had been filed and they would soon return to the safety of a Canadian builder's yard and leave at home.

The first assignment under their new skipper was to escort a large convoy from Milford Haven to Sheerness. A stiff gale spread the convoy over an area of 48 miles. The next day she met the convoy, with intense fog requiring the entire convoy to come to anchor off the Isle of Wight and wait for better visibility before completing the voyage safely.

Trentonian was then ordered into the Irish Sea to search for a German submarine that had been sighted. She returned to regular duties when the search was eventually called off.[36] During the early weeks of February 1945, *Trentonian*'s crew gave their ship a little love and attention, scraping the signs of age and hard work from her sides and applying a new coat of paint.

On 22 February 1945, *Trentonian* found herself as the sole escort of convoy BTC 76 from Bristol Channel to the Thames.[37] The day before, Glassco, along with the skipper of HMCS *Moose Jaw*, were called before the escort commander. He apologized to the two skippers and recognized the hard work by both crews and the two ships, but added that there was an escort job to be done and one ship had to do it. Both skippers, being gentlemen, volunteered for the job, and the debate was resolved with a simple toss of a coin. *Trentonian* won ... or lost, depending on your perspective.[38] With that they departed with a convoy of 10 ships in two columns of five. While at sea, the convoy was joined by a crane barge that had a Royal Navy motor launch as close escort.

Near Falmouth in the English Channel, *Trentonian* was ahead of the convoy performing an anti-submarine sweep with her asdic, when at 1320 the second ship in the port column exploded. This was the Liberty ship *Alexander Kennedy*.[39]

The officer-of-the-watch sounded "action stations" and gave the order "hard to port" on the wheel to turn the ship toward the suspected submarine, while at the same time the asdic operator gained a submerged contact on the starboard side of the convoy. Glassco arrived on the bridge immediately on hearing the explosion. After communicating with the convoy commodore, it was realized that the merchant ship had been torpedoed on her starboard side.

Glassco ordered *Trentonian* to complete her turn to avoid the rest of the convoy and the now sinking *Alexander Kennedy*.

As *Trentonian* cleared the ships of the convoy, the asdic contact was regained, and the skipper made the ship ready for a depth charge attack, dashing in to sink the U-boat.

At 1330 a loud explosion was felt throughout the ship and *Trentonian* gave an ominous shudder, slew sideways, and came to a stop, dead in the water.[40] She had been hit by a torpedo on the starboard side near the engine room. The explosion was so great the forward gun crew had to take cover from falling debris blown off the stern of the ship.[41]

The executive officer, Lieutenant Kinsman, went aft to investigate the damage. He reported back to the skipper that the boiler room and engine room were already flooding and the ship could not be saved. *Trentonian* began to settle by the stern, and Kinsmen gave the order, *"Stand by boats and floats*

and prepare to abandon ship!"[42] Her crew immediately went to work; the whaler was swung out and lowered, Carley floats slid into the water, and depth charges were made safe with the fuses tossed over the side. The navigating officer secured the code books into the weighted bag and tossed it too over the side. The crew then took up their positions for abandoning ship while some of the wounded were helped into the whaler. During this organized chaos, one of the ratings took off his sea boots and neatly placed them under a storage locker as if expecting to retrieve them later.[43] As their ship was slipping out from under them, the crew made ready in a calm and orderly fashion, each man performing his duty.

Glassco gave the order "ABANDON SHIP!" as her bow came out of the water. Kinsmen was second last to leave the ship, followed by the skipper as he calmly stepped from *Trentonian's* bridge into the English Channel, now at the same height as her bridge.[44] At 1340 the ship's hull became perpendicular to the water and she slipped in, stern first.[45]

HMCS *Trentonian* was gone.

It took just 14 minutes from the time the torpedo struck *Trentonian* until she was lost. The remaining wounded were pulled into the whaler while the rest hung onto the floats. To raise morale and keep the men occupied, they sang songs during the 45 minutes it took for rescue to start picking up the survivors, some so cold they could not lift themselves into the rescue boat.[46]

Five of her crew was lost with the ship. A sixth, an officer, would die in the lifeboat waiting for rescue. The remaining 95 of *Trentonian's* crew would be rescued, with two seriously wounded and 11 slightly wounded.[47]

The order to wear lifejackets, so unpopular with the crew a month earlier, proved to be a saving grace for them. The men who were killed died of the explosion from the torpedo, while none of *Trentonian's* crew was lost from drowning or the sinking of the ship. This one simple order is credited with saving many lives.

The German submarine was *U-1004*, on the second patrol of her career. She was commissioned into the German Navy only a few days from *Trentonian's* own commissioning date. *Trentonian* and *Alexander Kennedy* woud be her only two successes. There were 18 survivors rescued from *Alexander Kennedy*, with the loss of one life: Lamp Trimmer Alexander Tait.[48] *U-1004* survived the war and eventually surrendered to British forces, later being scuttled with the other remaining U-boats.

The survivors were landed at Falmouth, and with his shipmates attending the service, Lieutenant Stephen was buried in the local cemetery. The crew was then transferred by train to the Canadian Navy manning depot in Scotland to await survivors' leave. Their uniforms destroyed or lost, they were all given dark overalls to wear for the trip. When the train pulled into the station in London and the was crew taken off, the civilians nearby started to jeer and yell at them, calling them some despicable names including "Jerry" and "Nazi." It turned out that a prisoner of war train had passed through previously, and the POWs were dressed in similar clothing.[49]

The inquest into the sinking of *Trentonian* absolved Glassco of all blame and found no fault with his actions. The report goes on to say, "The conduct of the Officers and men appears to have been of the highest order …" The torpedo was probably not meant for *Trentonian*, but one of the merchant ships in the convoy. The report also explains the damage received to the ship, causing her to sink, "*Trentonian* was hit in her starboard quarter in the shaft tunnel which split the after engine room bulkhead, rapidly flooding up the after end of the ship. The watertight integrity of the ship was not affected, but this was sufficient to sink the ship by the stern until finally the boiler room flooded down through the fan casing."[50]

The skipper did receive a bit of a scare when he was directed to the inquest room, walking in to find it set up for a formal court martial. It turned out the petty officer had directed him to the wrong room by mistake.[51]

It was not until 26 March 1945 that the news of *Trentonian's* loss was made public by the censors, and the residents of Trenton learned of their ship's fate the same way as all Canadian's did — in a newspaper article. The news hit the community hard. Mayor Cory ordered the flags of the city be lowered to half-mast in honour of the men killed and the loss of the ship. He also sent a telegram to Lieutenant Glassco:

> Just heard news of sinking of *Trentonian* with loss of one officer and five ratings, also heroic attitude of the men during the ordeal. Trenton is proud of the record of her ship and crew which has been followed by the citizens, mourns with the families of the brave boys who were lost, and rejoice with those who were saved.

> Signed,
> H.R. Cory
> Mayor of the Town of Trenton[52]

Over the next few weeks, as the crew returned to Canada on survivors' leave, reports and letters were received in Trenton detailing the actions of the crew that fateful day. Some of the newspaper accounts listed how the biggest complaint of the men was the "wasted effort" of spending all that time painting the ship just before she was torpedoed.[53]

During her short career, HMCS *Trentonian* was well-supported by the city of Trenton. Citizens sent many packages to the ship, including hats, mitts, socks, magazines, books, stationery, food, ditty bags, wallets, record player, records, and musical instruments, just to name a few. Two large items were also sent to the ship: a washing machine and piano. The crew would later remark to the citizens of the city about just how important these gifts were to them and how appreciative they were.

Trenton's support of the ship did not end with her sinking, and the men in hospital continued to receive parcels while recovering. The packages that did not make it to the ship were forwarded to HMCS *Joliette*, because they were addressed to Lieutenant Commander Harrison, and the items were distributed to his crew.[54]

The local newspaper printed an article a few weeks after the loss of *Trentonian*; the article discussed the actions of the men, the record of the ship, the affection and attention from the citizens of Trenton, and the everlasting bond between the crew and the community. The final sentence of the article simply and powerfully stated these feelings:

> Trenton — yes all of Canada is proud
> of them, for they upheld the finest
> traditions of the navy.[55]

KILLED OR MISSING[56]

Honour Roll

HMCS TRENTONIAN

22 February 1945

BECK,
Moyle Kitchener
Leading Seaman, RCNR
Lunenburg, Nova Scotia
Age 28 years

CATHRINE,
Robert Thomas
Able Seaman, RCNVR
Windsor, Ontario
Age 19 years

FOURNIER,
John Alfred
Leading Seaman, RCNVR
Windsor, Ontario
Age 21 years

HARVEY,
Colin Bancroft
Leading Seaman, RCNR
Seal Cove, New Brunswick
Age 23 years

McCORMICK,
John
Stoker, RCNVR
Belleville, Ontario
Age 19 years

STEPHEN,
Gordon Kent
Lieutenant, RCNVR
Toronto, Ontario
Age 24 years

Chart prepared by Roger Litwiller

WOUNDED[57]

Atkinson, Sidney Charles _____ Vancouver, BC

Baril, William Richard _____ Trail, BC

Brako, Lawrence Douglas _____ Minnedosa, MB

Campbell, Hector Douglas _____ Ottawa, ON

Guthrie, George Walter _____ Regina, SK

Hadley, Vincent Earnest _____ Prince Albert, SK

Hanson, Odell Lorne _____ Nipawin, SK

Karns, Lewis Charles _____ London, ON

MacIver, Alexander John _____ Winnipeg, MB

Meyer, Peter Barrington _____ Regina, SK

Murphy, Lewis Joseph _____ Moose Jaw, SK

Rickard, James Allen _____ Port Arthur, ON

Thorogood, Edwin _____ Brantford, ON

SURVIVORS[58]

OFFICERS

Glassco, Colin Stinson, Lieutenant, RCNVR,
   Commanding Officer _____ Hamilton, ON

Kinsmen, William Burley, Lieutenant, RCNVR,
   Executive Officer _____ Vancouver, BC

Abbott, Ralph Patrick, Lieutenant, RCNVR,
   Navigating Officer _____ Oakville, ON

Dodds, Donald Jackson, Lieutenant, RCNVR,
   _____ Westmount, PQ

Mowat, James Keith, Acting Lieutenant, RCNVR,
   _____ Westmount, PQ

Hindle, Hamilton Francis, Warrant Officer, RCN,
   Engineer Officer _____ Vancouver, BC

MEN[59]

NEWFOUNDLAND

Bennett, Rupert Stanley _____ Conception Bay

PRINCE EDWARD ISLAND

Dye, Harry _____ Summerside

NOVA SCOTIA

Chadbolt, George _____ Halifax

Farmer, James Keith _____ New Glasgow

Johnston, Ross Allison _____ Halifax

Nolan, Lee Fraser _____ Halifax

Roberts, Donald Osborne _____ Derbert Station

Roberts, Thomas Raymond _____ Halifax

Roden, Bernard Gerald Joseph _____ Halifax

Walsh, William Francis _____ Newport

NEW BRUNSWICK

Eldridge, Gilbert Edwin _____ Beaver Harbour

QUEBEC

Barber, Walter Thomas _____ St. Lambert

Barron, Frank Henry _____ Montreal

Chapman, Isaie _____ Hull

Farrell, Thomas Philip _____ Montreal

Hayward, George Albert _____ Montreal

Kevins, Philip Anthony _____ Verdun

McKay, John Clifford _____ Terrebonne

ONTARIO

Angus, Murray Ross _____ Smith Falls

Bateman, Earl Douglas _____ Cobalt

Beaumon, Delmar Stanley _____ Glen Williams

Beer, Writer Jack _____ Toronto

Bergin, Michael George _____ Ottawa

Clark, Henry Alexander _____ King

Crampton, Norman Benjamin _____ Carleton Place

Davidson, James Archibald _____ Gatchell

Erwin, Robert J. _____ Toronto

Gibbons, Gordon _____ Acton

Goar, George Harvey _____ Toronto

Grey, Robert William _____ Toronto

Grigor, Alexander _____ London

Harley, Gordon _____ Hamilton

Holden, John _____ Windsor

Jacobs, William David _____ Ottawa

Keir, Bruce Dunston _____ Toronto

Majoros, Leslie _____ Hamilton

Eric Edward _____ Toronto

McIntyre, Norman _____ Hilton Beach

Poulin, Edmund Joseph _____ Ottawa

Runtz, Weldon Walter _____ Arnprior

Salmon, Harold Keith _____ Hamilton

Scott, John Richardson _____ Port Arthur

Shanahan, John Charles _____ Clinton

Shields, William Noel _____ Oakville

Simpson, Gordon Thomas _____ Toronto

Straw, Jack Eugene _____ Hamilton

Terrell, John William _____ Toronto

Vak, Michael _____ Port Arthur

Yakowenko, Joseph _____ London

MANITOBA

Gosskie, Joseph Edward _____ Birnie

Johnson, Russell Arden _____ Clanwilliam

Karbonic, Stanley Lawrence _____ East Kildonan

Kresko, John _____ Transcona

Slater, Arthur Bernard _____ Winnipeg

Robertson, Thomas W. _____ Winnipeg

SASKATCHEWAN

Baker, Elmer Bernard _____ Tribune

Cochran, Maurice Edward _____ Ratener

Evans, Roy _____ Saskatoon

McLaughlin, George Robert _____ Saskatoon

Powell, Robert James _____ Portreeve

Saretzky, Leo Bernard _____ Richlea

Singleton, Allan Egerton _____ Saskatoon

Taylor, Robert Creighton _____ Weyburn

ALBERTA

Coates, Sidney John _____ Carbon

Starr, Charles R. _____ Calgary

BRITISH COLUMBIA

Brennan, Bernard Benjamin _____ Victoria

Butler, Thomas Walter _____ Vancouver

Excell, Douglas _____ New Westminster

Gurr, Patrick Charles _____ Kelowna

Lounsbury, Raymond _____ Vancouver

Medhurst, Richard Paul _____ Victoria

Miner, Reginald Allen _____ Vancouver

Roy, Robert Alex _____ Vancouver

Sharpe, Norman Henry _____ Vancouver

Thompson, Wilfred Bruce _____ Vancouver

BRITISH WEST INDIES

Graham, Darcy Hamel _____ San Juan, Trinidad

AWARDS EARNED BY CREW:

- Harrison, William Edward, Acting Temporary Lieutenant-Commander, RCNVR: Distinguished Service Cross (DSC)

  The King has been graciously pleased on the Occasion of the Celebration of His Majesty's Birthday to give orders for the following awards for gallantry or outstanding service in the face of the enemy, or for zeal, patience and cheerfulness in dangerous waters, and for setting an example of wholehearted devotion to duty upholding the high tradition of the Royal (Canadian) Navy.

- Excell, Douglas, Engine Room Artificer Fourth Class, RCNVR: Mention in Dispatches (MID)

  Following the torpedoing of his ship HMCS Trentonian, this rating remained behind at risk of his own life to assist in the removal of the wounded men from the quarterdeck. This action is in keeping with the highest traditions of the Royal Canadian Navy.

- Goar, George, Acting Engine Room Artificer, RCNR: Mention in Dispatches (MID)

  After the torpedoing of HMCS Trentonian, this rating showed extreme courage in helping the wounded survivors from the ship to a Carley float, and then took charge of the party until rescue was effected. Although a non-swimmer, he showed disregard for his own safety throughout. His bravery and gallantry are well worthy of commendation.

- Hindle, Hamilton Francis, RCN, Warrant Engineer: Mention in Dispatches (MID)

  As engineer Officer of HMCS Trentonian when she was torpedoed in February, 1945, Mr. Hindle displayed integrity and zeal to a marked degree. In clearing the engine room of all its personnel after the order "Abandon Ship" had been given, he remained until the last moment without thought of personal risk.

- Kinsman, William Burnley, Lieutenant, RCNVR: Mention in Dispatches (MID)

  At the time of the sinking of HMCS Trentonian this officer's conduct was of the highest order. He remained cool as he organized the men when the order to "Abandon Ship" was given. Later, from the ship's whaler, Lieutenant Kinsman picked up survivors and saw to it that the injured were placed aboard one of His Majesty's Canadian M.L.'s which was in the vicinity.

Commanding Officers

William E. Harrison, LCDR, RCNR	1 December 1943 to 30 January 1945
Colin S. Glassco, LT, RCNVR	31 January 1945 to 22 February 1945

HMCS *TRENTONIAN*
BATTLE HONOURS

ATLANTIC	1944
ENGLISH CHANNEL	1944–1945
NORMANDY	1944

Specifications

Name:	HMCS *Trentonian*, alternate name for the city of Trenton		
Classification:	Revised Flower class, increased endurance, 1942–1943 program		
Builder:	Kingston Shipbuilding Company Limited — Kingston, Ontario		
Keel Laid: 19/02/43	Launched: 01/09/43	Commissioned: 01/12/43	Paid off: 22/02/45
Length: 208 feet, 4 inches		Beam: 33 feet, 1 inch	Draught: 11 feet
Displacement: 970 tons	Speed: 16 knots	Endurance: 7,400 nautical miles at 10 knots	Fuel: 338 tons
Crew: 7 officers, 90 other ranks	Machinery: 4 cycle triple expansion engine, two water tube boilers		
Armament:	- one 4 inch QF Mk. XIX gun — forward gun platform - one 12-pdr. pom-pom gun — after gun tub - two single 20 mm Oerlikon machine guns — bridge wings - four single 20 mm Oerlikon machine guns (added before transit to UK) — 2 waist/2 aft of gun tub - one Hedgehog anti-submarine mortar — forward gun platform - four depth charge throwers — waist - depth charge rails — stern - 100 depth charges		

Chart prepared by Roger Litwiller.

Specifications of HMCS Trentonian.

EPILOGUE

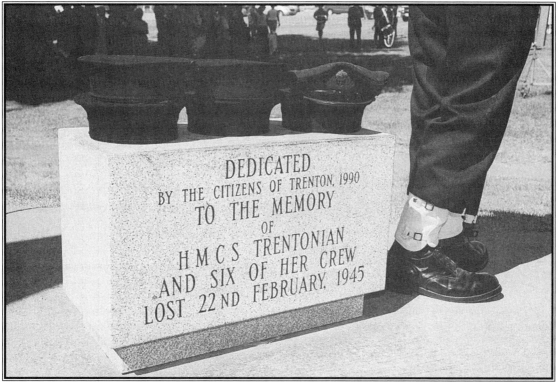

Photo courtesy Corporal Jim Jordan, 8 Wing, CFB Trenton Imaging Section.

The cenotaph in Trenton has a memorial stone dedicated to HMCS Trentonian *and the six men killed when she was torpedoed and sunk on 22 February 1945. This picture was taken during the last reunion of her crew in 2002. A sailor's cap was placed on the memorial stone by a survivor of* Trentonian, *in memory of each man killed. The officer's cap is from the Glassco family and is reported to have been worn by Lieutenant Glassco as he stepped from* Trentonian's *bridge into the English Channel as his ship sank beneath him.*

THE STORY OF THESE SHIPS DOES NOT end with their decommissioning and eventual scrapping — each community has kept the story of these ships alive. In several locations in the communities are displays, plaques, and memorials giving tribute to the memory of these ships and the actions of their crews.

Their names may no longer be attached to a serving warship, but several of those mentioned have had sea cadets and navy league cadet corps take them as their own, keeping the history of the ships alive. Soon after joining one of these cadet corps, a cadet is told the history of their namesake ship and quickly learns why there is such pride in the name. On occasion, a crewmember of the ship will be invited to the corps and the cadets experience firsthand the story of their ship.

The communities themselves have endeavoured to keep contact with the ships. The Trenton branch of the Royal Canadian Legion and the City of Trenton have hosted several reunions for *Trentonian's* crew. The last reunion was in 2002. Twelve members

Photo courtesy Catherine Ruta.

Members of the Naval Reserve Unit, HMCS Cataraqui, *present the mayor of Napanee, Gordon Schermerhorn, with the plaque honouring HMCS* Napanee *and her relationship with the city, during the 2010 Canadian Naval Centennial celebrations and the Freedom of the City Parade.*

Photo courtesy Rhonda Litwiller.

Four members of HMCS Trentonian's *crew unveil the plaque presented to the city of Trenton during the 2010 Canadian Naval Centennial celebration in Trenton. Pictured from left to right: Gordon Gibbins, Jim Erwin, Bill Shields, (not visible is Eric Muff).*

of *Trentonian*'s crew were able to attend, and the highlight of the weekend was a parade and memorial service involving almost 200 naval personnel, two navy bands, and an air force band. This was an incredible event for a community that is now known for the air force alone.

The 100th anniversary of the Canadian Navy was celebrated in 2010. As part of the celebrations, Canada's navy presented every community that had a ship named for it with a plaque commemorating the service of the ship and renewing the relationship between the community and the navy.

The local naval reserve unit in Kingston, HMCS *Cataraqui* was responsible for the communities in the Bay of Quinte area. The scope of the presentations was left to be decided upon by the individual communities, and in this region the renewed partnership with the Navy was welcomed with excitement, enthusiasm, and pride.

Napanee had a large celebration with a freedom of the city parade for the local sea cadet corps, RCSCC Napanee, and Prince Edward County invited HMCS *Cataraqui* to the New Year's Levee in Picton. The city of Belleville had a special presentation ceremony following a seminar on how to preserve our history.

Quinte West, which now includes Trenton, hosted a reception near the anniversary of *Trentonian*'s loss. Four of *Trentonian*'s crew who survived her sinking were present for the presentation of the plaque to the city.

In each of these areas, the plaques and the presentation materials have been included in the displays and memorials of the ships, adding another chapter to the history of the associated ship and community.

History itself is a living, evolving series of events, continuously being added to and rewritten. As our veterans come forward, the story grows. A small recollection can form the basis of an interesting story. This is why it is so important to keep a record of all that we do: today's scrapbooks will become tomorrow's stories that make our history interesting.

Although no longer the four-hundred-ship force it was at the end of the Second World War, Canada's navy remains strong and active, serving in many operations throughout the world. The navy has continued the tradition of naming ships for Canadian communities, and maybe, someday, as new ships are constructed, the names of *Belleville*, *Hallowell*, *Quinte*, *Napanee*, or *Trentonian* will once again be given to an active Canadian warship.

NOTES

CHAPTER 2 — HMCS *NAPANEE*

1. Ken Macpherson, "Naval Shipbuilding on the Great Lakes, 1940–45," *FreshWater — A Journal of Great Lakes Marine History*, Vol. 3, No. 1, 1988; Maurice D. Smith, "Kingston Shipyards — World War II," *FreshWater — A Journal of Great Lakes Marine History*, Vol, 5 No. 1, 1990.

2. County of Lennox and Addington Museum and Archives, File HMCS *Napanee*.

3. Robert F. D. Hall (son of Mayor and Mrs. Hall) Collection.

4. *Ibid*.

5. *Ibid*.

6. County of Lennox and Addington Museum and Archives, File HMCS *Napanee*.

7. The Canadian Navy formed its personnel into three categories: the regular navy was RCN (Royal Canadian Navy), the reserve members were RCNR (Royal Canadian Naval Reserve), and volunteers for the duration of the war were RCNVR (Royal Canadian Naval Volunteer Reserve). The members of the RCNVR made up the largest number of men and were referred to as the "Wavy Navy," due to the wave pattern of the officers' rank braid.

8. Department of National Defence, Directorate of History and Heritage, HMCS *Napanee* — File 81/520/8000, Box 67, File 7, History of HMCS *Napanee*.

9. County of Lennox and Addington Museum and Archives, File HMCS *Napanee*.

10. Department of National Defence, Directorate of History and Heritage, HMCS *Napanee* — File 81/520/8000, Box 67, File 7, Ship's Movements.

11. Department of National Defence, Directorate of History and Heritage, HMCS *Napanee* — File 81/520/8000, Box 67, File 7.

12. German submarines would patrol an area until they spotted a convoy. The U-boat would then shadow the convoy and report its location to German Naval Headquarters, who would in turn direct other U-boats to the area. Once all of the U-boats were assembled, they would attack in mass, forming a "wolf pack" as they hunted their prey.

13. As a side note, the ship that Lieutenant Commander Dobson took command of was HMCS *St. Croix*. Under his command the destroyer led a very successful career, sinking several U-boats. Unfortunately, *St. Croix* would be lost on 20 September 1943. She was torpedoed by *U-305*, using a new torpedo called a GNAT, which is an acoustic homing torpedo. Eighty-one of her crew were rescued by HMS *Itchen*, but three days later *Itchen* was also torpedoed, by *U-666*. There were only three survivors: two from *Itchen* and one from *St. Croix*. Lieutenant Commander Dobson was lost with the rest of his crew.

14. Library and Archives Canada, RG 24, Volume 6761, File NSS 8180-331/67, HMCS *Napanee* Collisions and Groundings.

15. Department of National Defence, Directorate of History and Heritage, HMCS *Napanee* — File 81/520/8000, Box 67, File 7, Ship's Movements and History of HMCS *Napanee*.

16. Department of National Defence, Directorate of History and Heritage, HMCS *Napanee* — File 81/520/8000, Box 67, File 7, Ship's Movements.

17. County of Lennox and Addington Museum and Archives, File HMCS *Napanee*; Department of National Defence, Directorate of History and Heritage, HMCS *Napanee* — File 81/520/8000, Box 67, File 7, History of HMCS *Napanee*.

18. Department of National Defence, Directorate of History and Heritage, HMCS *Napanee* — File 81/520/8000, Box 67, File 7, Ship's Movements and History of HMCS *Napanee*.

19. County of Lennox and Addington Museum and Archives, File HMCS *Napanee*.

20. Department of National Defence, Directorate of History and Heritage, HMCS *Napanee* — File 81/520/8000, Box 67, File 7, Ship's Movements.

21. Letter sequence given to convoys starting from the north of the United Kingdom and proceeding to North America.

22. The "S" designation is for Slow convoy.

23. ASDIC is an acronym for Allied Submarine Detection and Investigation Committee; we know it now by the more common term, *sonar*.

24. Library and Archives Canada, RG 24, Volume 6761, File NSS 8180-331/67, HMCS *Napanee* Collisions and Groundings.

25. Letter sequence given to convoys starting from United Kingdom to the Mediterranean, with the "S" designating a Slow convoy.

26. HMCS *St. Croix* was senior officer of the escort group C1 under command of Lieutenant Commander Dobson, *Napanee*'s first commanding officer.

27. Letter sequence given to convoy starting from Mediterranean to the United Kingdom, with the "S" designating a Slow convoy.

28. Some reference books give credit to both *Prescott* and *Napanee* for sinking *U-163*, while others give credit solely to *Prescott*.

29. Department of National Defence, Directorate of History and Heritage, HMCS *Napanee* — File 81/520/8000, Box 67, File 7, History of HMCS *Napanee*.

30. Department of National Defence, Directorate of History and Heritage, HMCS *Napanee* — File 81/520/8000, Box 67, File 7, History of HMCS *Napanee*.

31. Library and Archives Canada, RG 24, Volume 6761, File NSS 8180-331/67, HMCS *Napanee* Collisions and Groundings.

32. *Ibid.*

33. Department of National Defence, Directorate of History and Heritage, HMCS *Napanee* — File 81/520/8000, Box 67, File 7, Ship's Movements.

34. Library and Archives Canada, RG 24, Volume 11563, File D.15-2-3 HMCS *Napanee*, Collisions and Groundings — Message.

35. Library and Archives Canada, RG 24, Volume 11563, File D.15-2-3 HMCS *Napanee*, Collisions and Groundings — Letter, W.L. Puxley, Acting Captain (RN), Captain (D), Halifax.

36. Library and Archives Canada, RG 24, Volume 6761, File NSS 8180-331/67, HMCS *Napanee*, Collisions and Groundings — Letter, L.W. Murray, Rear Admiral, Commander-in-Chief, Canadian Northwest Atlantic.

37. Department of National Defence, Directorate of History and Heritage, HMCS *Napanee* — File 81/520/8000, Box 67, File 7, History of HMCS *Napanee*.

38. IODE: International Order of the Daughters of the Empire — Mrs. Hall was the local chapter's Regent. Robert F. D. Hall (son of Mayor and Mrs. Hall) Collection.

39. *Ibid.*

40. *Ibid.*

CHAPTER 3 — HMCS *BELLEVILLE*

1. Maurice D. Smith, "Kingston Shipyards — World War II," *FreshWater — A Journal of Great Lakes Marine History*, Vol. 5, No. 1, 1990.

2. *The Ontario Intelligencer*, Belleville, Ontario, 23 October 1944.

3. *The Ontario Intelligencer*, Belleville, Ontario, 23 October 1944. Approval for HMCS *Belleville* to visit the city of Belleville had been given on 2 October 1944. There is no factual evidence that the ship visited the city. The newspaper account is very clear on the location of the adoption ceremony and the date it took place. In order for a corvette to visit Belleville it would have to travel through the narrow channel east of Belleville in the Bay of Quinte, as well as contend with the lack of water depth in Belleville itself.

4. Library and Archives Canada, RG 24, Volume 6809, File NSC 8700-332/12, HMCS *Belleville* — Movements.

5. Library and Archives Canada, RG 24, Volume 6809, File NSC 8700-332/12, HMCS *Belleville* — Movements.

6. Department of National Defence, Directorate of History and Heritage, HMCS *Belleville* — File 81/520/8000, Box 81, File 2, Report of Proceedings, 18 January to 20 January.

7. Library and Archives Canada, RG 24, Volume 6809, File NSC 8700-332/12, HMCS *Belleville* — Movements.

8. *Ibid.*

9. *Ibid.*

10. Department of National Defence, Directorate of History and Heritage, HMCS *Belleville* — File 81/520/8000, Box 81, File 2, Movements.

11. Department of National Defence, Directorate of History and Heritage, HMCS *Belleville* — File 81/520/8000, Box 81, File 2, Press Release, 11 June 1945.

12. *Ibid.*

13. Department of National Defence, Directorate of History and Heritage, HMCS *Belleville* — File 81/520/8000, Box 81, File 2, Movements.

14. *Ibid.*

15. Library and Archives Canada, RG 24, Volume 6809, File NSC 8700-332/12, HMCS *Belleville* — Movements.

16. RCSCC *Quinte* — File HMCS *Belleville*.

CHAPTER 4 — HMCS *HALLOWELL*

1. Department of National Defence, Directorate of History and Heritage, HMCS *Hallowell* — File 81/520/8000, Box 45, File 2, *Halifax Mail Star*, "Naval Hero's Birthplace — An Unsettled Argument," 19 February 1960.

2. *Picton Gazette*, "Sir Benjamin Hallowell Fought Under Nelson," 19 July 1944.

3. *Picton Gazette*, "Frigate Launched at Montreal Given Name of Hallowell," 5 April 1944.

4. Department of National Defence, Directorate of History and Heritage, HMCS *Hallowell* — File 81/520/8000, Box 45, File 2, Herald, 29 March 1944.

5. *Picton Gazette*, "5 Boats in 24 Hours is Montreal Record", 31 March 1944.

6. *Picton Gazette*, "Officer of HMCS *Hallowell* Awarded the George Medal," 19 August 1944.

7. *Picton Gazette*, "I.O.D.E. to Buy Ship's Bell for Frigate Hallowell," 12 April 1944.

8. Library and Archives Canada, RG 24, Volume 11561, File 8-23-3, HMCS *Hallowell* — Naval Message.

9. Library and Archives Canada, RG 24, Volume 11111, File 55-2-1/483, HMCS *Hallowell* — Memorandum.

10. Library and Archives Canada, RG 24, Volume 6763, File NSC 8180-381/16, HMCS *Hallowell* — Memorandum to Hydrographer.

11. Library and Archives Canada, RG 24, Volume 11111, File 55-2-1/483, HMCS *Hallowell* — HMCS *Somer Isle*.

12. MAC ships were Merchant Aircraft Carriers — merchant ships built to carry aircraft to assist in the protection of the convoy from submarines.

13. Maritime Command Museum — File HMCS *Hallowell*.

14. Department of National Defence, Directorate of History and Heritage, HMCS *Hallowell* — File 81/520/8000, Box 45, File 2, Report of Proceedings of Escort Group C.1.

15. Department of National Defence, Directorate of History and Heritage, HMCS *Hallowell* — File 81/520/8000, Box 45, File 2, *Hallowell*, Frigate, River C. 8.8.44.

16. Maritime Command Museum, File HMCS *Hallowell*.

17. Department of National Defence, Directorate of History and Heritage, HMCS *Hallowell* — File 81/520/8000, Box 45, File 2, A History of the Frigates HMCS *Strathadam*, *Hallowell*, *Violetta*.

CHAPTER 5 — HMCS *QUINTE*

1. Department of National Defence, Directorate of History and Heritage, HMCS *Quinte* — File 81/520/8000, Box 85, File 6.

2. *Ibid.*

3. Department of National Defence, Directorate of History and Heritage, HMCS *Quinte* — File 81/520/8000, Box 85, File 6, Ship Movements.

4. Royal Canadian Sea Cadet Corps Quinte, Belleville — File HMCS *Quinte*, Ship's History.

5. HMCS *Clayoquot* had a successful career during the war. Unfortunately, she met a most tragic fate: she was torpedoed and sunk by the German submarine *U-806*, three miles from the Sambro Light vessel just outside of Halifax harbor, during the night of the last Christmas Eve of the war, 24 December 1944. Eight of her crew were lost with her.

6. Department of National Defence, Directorate of History and Heritage, HMCS *Quinte* — File 81/520/8000, Box 85, File 6, Ship Movements.

7. *Ibid.*

8. *Ibid.*

9. Department of National Defence, Directorate of History and Heritage, HMCS *Quinte* — File 81/520/8000, Box 85, File 6, A Brief History of HMCS *Quinte*, First of Name.

10. Department of National Defence, Directorate of History and Heritage, HMCS *Quinte* — File 81/520/8000, Box 85, File 6, Ship Movements.

11. Department of National Defence, Directorate of History and Heritage, HMCS *Quinte* — File 81/520/8000, Box 85, File 6, Message.

12. Department of National Defence, Directorate of History and Heritage, HMCS *Quinte* — File 81/520/8000, Box 85, File 6, Report of Proceedings.

13. Department of National Defence, Directorate of History and Heritage, HMCS *Quinte* — File 81/520/8000, Box 85, File 6, Letter to Director of Operations Division.

14. *Ibid.*

15. Library and Archives Canada, RG 24, Volume 11108, File 55-2-1/175 — Grounding of HMCS *Quinte*.

16. *Ibid.*

17. *Ibid.*

18. *Ibid.*

19. NOIC: Naval Officer In Charge.

20. Department of National Defence, Directorate of History and Heritage, HMCS *Quinte* — File 81/520/8000, Box 85, File 6, A Brief History of HMCS *Quinte*, First of Name.

21. *Ibid.*

22. Library and Archives Canada, RG 24, Volume 6766, File NS18180-443/51 — Collisions and Groundings HMCS *Napanee*, Letter Foundation Maritime Limited.

23. *Ibid.*

24. Department of National Defence, Directorate of History and Heritage, HMCS *Quinte* — File 81/520/8000, Box 85, File 6, Letter to Director of Operations Division.

25. Department of National Defence, Directorate of History and Heritage, HMCS *Quinte* — File 81/520/8000, Box 85, File 6, Groundings and Collisions.

26. Department of National Defence, Directorate of History and Heritage, HMCS *Quinte* — File

81/520/8000, Box 85, File 6.

27. Department of National Defence, Directorate of History and Heritage, HMCS *Quinte* — File 81/520/8000, Box 85, File 6, Groundings and Collisions.

28. *Ibid.*

29. Department of National Defence, Directorate of History and Heritage, HMCS *Quinte* — File 81/520/8000, Box 85, File 6, A Brief History of HMCS *Quinte*, First of Name.

30. Library and Archives Canada, RG 24, Volume 6766, File NS18180-443/51 — Collisions and Groundings HMCS *Quinte*, Report Commanding Officer.

31. Department of National Defence, Directorate of History and Heritage, HMCS *Quinte* — File 81/520/8000, Box 85, File 6, Naval Message 12/02/45.

32. Library and Archives Canada, RG 24, Volume 6766, File NS18180-443/51 — Collisions and Groundings, HMCS *Quinte*, Survey HMCS *Quinte*.

33. Department of National Defence, Directorate of History and Heritage, HMCS *Quinte* — File 81/520/8000, Box 85, File 6, A Brief History of HMCS *Quinte*, First of Name.

Chapter 6 — HMCS *Quinte*(II)

1. Department of National Defence, Directorate of History and Heritage, HMCS *Quinte* (II) — File 81/520/8000, Box 85, File 7, A Brief Narrative of HMCS *Quinte*, Second of Name.

2. Department of National Defence, Directorate of History and Heritage, HMCS *Quinte* (II) — File 81/520/8000, Box 85, File 7, Press Release, Launching Arrangements, AMC 149.

3. Thunder Bay Public Library Archives, The Fort William *Daily Times-Journal*, "Minesweeper *Quinte* Launched," 10 August 1953.

4. Thunder Bay Public Library Archives, The Fort William *Daily Times-Journal*, "Shipyard to Build Second Naval Ship," 10 August 1953.

5. Thunder Bay Public Library Archives, The Fort William *Daily Times-Journal*, "Warship Ceremony Is Held," 15 October 1954.

6. Department of National Defence, Directorate of History and Heritage, HMCS *Quinte* (II) — File 81/520/8000, Box 85, File 7, Press Release, 13 October 1954.

7. Department of National Defence, Directorate of History and Heritage, HMCS *Quinte* (II) — File 81/520/8000, Box 85, File 7, Announcement by Naval Headquarters, 17 May 1957.

8. National Archives of Canada, NAVY 4193, File 9430-MSC 149 — Fire Report 16 October 1954, HMCS *Quinte*.

9. Department of National Defence, Directorate of History and Heritage, HMCS *Quinte* (II) — File 81/520/8000, Box 85, File 7, A Brief Narrative of HMCS *Quinte*, Second of Name.

10. Department of National Defence, Directorate of History and Heritage, HMCS *Quinte* (II) — File 81/520/8000, Box 85, File 7, A Brief Narrative of HMCS *Quinte*, Second of Name.

11. Department of National Defence, Directorate of History and Heritage, HMCS *Quinte* (II) — File 81/520/8000, Box 85, File 8, Monthly Report, June 1956.

12. Library and Archives Canada, RG 24, Volume 4101, File 1151-FSE 169, Boards of Enquiry and Investigations — Collisions, Groundings and Damage, Collision of HMCS *Portage* with HMCS *Quinte*, Statement of LCDR D.P. Brownlow.

13. Library and Archives Canada, RG 24, Volume 4101, File 1151-FSE 169, Boards of Enquiry and Investigations — Collisions, Groundings and Damage, Collision of HMCS *Portage* with HMCS *Quinte*.

14. Library and Archives Canada, RG 24, Volume 4101, File 1151-FSE 169, Boards of Enquiry and Investigations — Collisions, Groundings and Damage, Collision of HMCS *Portage* with HMCS *Quinte*, Report of the Board of Inquiry.

15. Library and Archives Canada, NAVY 4193, File 9430-MSC 149, Fire Report, 3 March 1957, HMCS *Quinte* 149.

16. Department of National Defence, Directorate of History and Heritage, HMCS *Quinte* (II) — File 81/520/8000, Box 85, File 8, Monthly Report, June 1957.

17. *Ibid.*

18. Department of National Defence, Directorate of History and Heritage, HMCS *Quinte* (II) — File 81/520/8000, Box 85, File 7, Press Release, 17 May 1957.

19. Department of National Defence, Directorate of History and Heritage, HMCS *Quinte* (II) — File 81/520/8000, Box 85, File 7, A Brief Narrative of HMCS *Quinte*, Second of Name.

20. *Ibid.*

21. *Ibid.*

22. Department of National Defence, Directorate of History and Heritage, HMCS *Quinte* (II) — File 81/520/8000, Box 85, File 8, Monthly Report of Proceedings, 31 March 1958.

23. Department of National Defence, Directorate of History and Heritage, HMCS *Quinte* (II) — File 81/520/8000, Box 85, File 8, *Halifax Chronicle-Herald*, 31 March 1958.

24. Department of National Defence, Directorate of History and Heritage, HMCS *Quinte* (II) — File 81/520/8000, Box 85, File 7, A Brief Narrative of HMCS *Quinte*, Second of Name.

25. *Ibid.*

26. Department of National Defence, Directorate of History and Heritage, HMCS *Quinte* (II) — File 81/520/8000, Box 85, File 8, Rescue Brings Commendation, Crowsnest, July 1959.

27. Department of National Defence, Directorate of History and Heritage, HMCS *Quinte* (II) — File 81/520/8000, Box 85, File 7, A Brief Narrative of HMCS *Quinte*, Second of Name.

28. *Ibid.*

29. *Ibid.*

30. *Ibid.*

31. *Ibid.*

32. Library and Archives Canada, NAVY 4193, File 9430-MSC 149, Fire Report, 25 November 1960, HMCS *Quinte* 149.

33. Department of National Defence, Directorate of History and Heritage, HMCS *Quinte* (II) — File 81/520/8000, Box 85, File 8, Commanding Officers Report, 8 December 1960.

34. Department of National Defence, Directorate of History and Heritage, HMCS *Quinte* (II) — File 81/520/8000, Box 85, File 7, Brief Narrative of HMCS *Quinte*, Second of Name.

35. The Fort William *Daily Times-Journal*, "Mine-sweeper Squadron Seen in Manoeuvres," 12 June 1961.

36. Department of National Defence, Directorate of History and Heritage, HMCS *Quinte* (II) — File 81/520/8000, Box 85, File 7, Brief Narrative of HMCS *Quinte*, Second of Name.

37. Department of National Defence, Directorate of History and Heritage, HMCS *Quinte* (II) — File 81/520/8000, Box 85, File 7, Press Release, Shipyards Given Big Job, 25 April 1962.

38. Department of National Defence, Directorate of History and Heritage, HMCS *Quinte* (II) — File 81/520/8000, Box 85, File 7, A Brief Narrative of HMCS *Quinte*, Second of Name.

39. *Ibid.*

40. *Ibid.*

41. Department of National Defence, Directorate of History and Heritage, HMCS *Quinte* (II) — File 81/520/8000, Box 85, File 8, Reports of Proceedings, Atlantic Command, November 1962.

42. Department of National Defence, Directorate of History and Heritage, HMCS *Quinte* (II) — File 81/520/8000, Box 85, File 7, A Brief Narrative of HMCS *Quinte*, Second of Name.

43. *Ibid.*

44. Department of National Defence, Directorate of History and Heritage, HMCS *Quinte* (II) — File 81/520/8000, Box 85, File 8, Report of Proceedings, HMCS *Quinte*, January 1964.

45. *Ibid.*

46. Department of National Defence, Directorate of History and Heritage, HMCS *Quinte* (II) — File 81/520/8000, Box 85, File 7, Information from Crown Assets, 15 December 1971.

47. Department of National Defence, Directorate of History and Heritage, HMCS *Quinte* (II) — File 81/520/8000, Box 85, File 7, A Brief Narrative of HMCS *Quinte*, Second of Name.

CHAPTER 7 — HMCS *TRENTONIAN*

1. Ken Macpherson, "Naval Shipbuilding on the Great Lakes, 1940–45," *FreshWater — A Journal of Great Lakes Marine History*, Vol. 3, No. 1, 1988

2. Jack Harold (RCNVR, Signalman; HMCS *Trentonian*) in discussion with the author, February 2002.

3. Hazel Farley Collection, Quinte West Public Library, Letter from W.E. Harrison, 17 December 1943.

4. Library and Archives Canada, RG 24, Volume 6911, File NSS 8970-332/109 — Working Up Programme, HMCS *Trentonian*.

5. Jack Harold (RCNVR, Signalman; HMCS *Trentonian*) in discussion with the author, February 2002.

6. Library and Archives Canada, RG 24, Volume 6911, File NSS 8970-332/109 — Working Up Programme, HMCS *Trentonian*.

7. Jack Harold (RCNVR, Signalman; HMCS *Trentonian*) in discussion with the author, February 2002.

8. Bruce Keir (RCNVR, Stoker; HMCS *Trentonian*) in discussion with the author, June 2000.

9. Library and Archives Canada, RG 24, Volume 11739, File CS 161-86-3 — Monthly Report of Proceedings, May 1944.

10. Bruce Keir (RCNVR, Stoker; HMCS *Trentonian*) in discussion with the author, June 2000.

11. Library and Archives Canada, RG 24, Volume 11739, File CS 161-86-3 — Monthly Report of Proceedings, May 1944.

12. *Ibid*.

13. Personal Collection of Jack Harold (RCNVR, Signalman; HMCS *Trentonian*).

14. Library and Archives Canada, RG 24, Volume 11739, File CS 161-86-3 — Monthly Report of Proceedings, June 1944.

15. Library and Archives Canada, RG 24, Volume 11739 File CS 161-86-1 — Engagement of HMTS *Monarch* by USS *Plunkett*.

16. Jack Harold (RCNVR, Signalman; HMCS *Trentonian*) in discussion with the author, February 2002.

17. Hazel Farley Collection, Quinte West Public Library, excerpt from letter from W.E. Harrison, 25 May 1944.

18. Jack Harold (RCNVR, Signalman; HMCS *Trentonian*) in discussion with the author, February 2002.

19. Library and Archives Canada, RG 24, Volume 11739 File CS 161-86-1 — Engagement of HMTS *Monarch* by USS *Plunkett*.

20. *Ibid*.

21. Ship's Log, USS *Plunkett*.

22. Ship's Log, USS *Plunkett*.

23. Library and Archives Canada, RG 24, Volume 11739 File CS 161-86-1 — Engagement of HMTS *Monarch* by USS *Plunkett*.

24. Department of National Defence, Directorate of History and Heritage, HMCS *Trentonian* — File 81/520/8000, Box 105, File 5, Newspaper Article, Ottawa *Journal*, Jack Macbeth: "American Destroyer's Gunfire Smashed Cableship Namesake," 19 December 1953.

25. Hazel Farley Collection, Quinte West Public Library, letter from W.E. Harrison, 11 July 1944.

26. Bruce Keir (RCNVR, Stoker; HMCS *Trentonian*) in discussion with the author, June 2000.

27. Library and Archives Canada, Volume 11739, File CS 161-86-1 — Monthly Report of Proceedings, September 1944.

28. Bruce Keir (RCNVR, Stoker; HMCS *Trentonian*) in discussion with the author, June 2000.

29. Library and Archives Canada, Volume 11739, File CS 161-86-1 — Report of Proceedings, Escort of Phoenix Convoy.

30. Hazel Farley Collection, Quinte West Public Library, letter from W.E. Harrison, 11 November 1944.

31. Bruce Keir (RCNVR, Stoker; HMCS *Trentonian*) in discussion with the author, June 2000.

32. Hazel Farley Collection, Quinte West Public Library, letter from W.E. Harrison, 6 January 1945.

33. Hazel Farley Collection, Quinte West Public Library, letter from W.E. Harrison, 25 January 1945.

34. Private Collection of Roger Glassco (son of Lieutenant Commander Colin Glassco, RCNVR).

35. City of Quinte West Public Library, The *Trentonian*, "Skipper Recalls *Trentonian* Sinking," 7 May 1979.

36. *Ibid.*

37. Library and Archives Canada, RG 24, Volume 6889, File NSS 8870-332/109 — Sinking of HMCS *Trentonian*.

38. Max Corkum (RCNVR, Navigating Officer; HMCS *Moose Jaw*) in discussion with the author, June 2000.

39. Library and Archives Canada, RG 24, Volume 6889, File NSS 8870-332/109 — Sinking of HMCS *Trentonian*.

40. *Ibid.*

41. Frank Barron (RCNVR, Gun Layer; HMCS *Trentonian*) in discussion with the author, March 2004.

42. Library and Archives Canada, RG 24, Volume 6889, File NSS 8870-332/109 — Sinking of HMCS *Trentonian*.

43. Gord Gibbins (HMCS *Trentonian*) in discussion with the author, July 2000.

44. Roger Glassco (son of Lieutenant Colin Glassco; HMCS *Trentonian*) in discussion with the author, July 2001.

45. Library and Archives Canada, RG 24, Volume 6889, File NSS 8870-332/109 — Sinking of HMCS *Trentonian*.

46. Library and Archives Canada, RG 24 Volume 11739, File CS 161-86-1 — Naval Message from FOIC Falmouth.

47. Library and Archives Canada, RG 24, Volume 6889, File NSS 8870-332/109 — Sinking of HMCS *Trentonian*.

48. Department of National Defence, Directorate of History and Heritage, HMCS *Trentonian* — File 81/520/8000, Box 105, File 5, Naval Message, 22 February 1945.

49. Bruce Keir (RCNVR, Stoker; HMCS *Trentonian*) in discussion with the author, June 2000.

50. Library and Archives Canada, RG 24, Volume 4107, File 1156-332/109 — Report, Board of Inquiry, Sinking of HMCS *Trentonian*.

51. Bruce Keir (RCNVR, Stoker; HMCS *Trentonian*) in discussion with the author, June 2000.

52. City of Quinte West Public Library, HMCS *Trentonian*, Hazel Farley Collection, Newspaper

Article, "Mayor Sends Cable to Commander on Citizens Behalf."

53. The *Hamilton Spectator*, "Survivors from *Trentonian* Bemoan Lost Coat of Paint," 26 March 1945.

54. City of Quinte West Public Library, HMCS *Trentonian*, Hazel Farley Collection, Magazines from Trenton on "Joliette."

55. City of Quinte West Public Library, HMCS *Trentonian*, Hazel Farley Collection, Article, "The Men Were Marvelous."

56. Navy League Cadet Corps Trentonian, File HMCS *Trentonian*, Honour Roll.

57. Library and Archives Canada, RG 24, Volume 11755, File HMCS *Trentonian* — List of Survivors, HMCS *Trentonian*.

58. *Ibid.*

59. *Ibid.*

GLOSSARY OF ABBREVIATIONS AND TERMS

AA	Anti-Aircraft	**Capt.**	Captain, Air Force or Army
AB	Able Seaman	**Capt(N)**	Captain, Navy
Aft	Toward the rear of a ship	**CAT**	Canadian Anti-acoustic Torpedo Device
A/S	Anti Submarine		
A/SLt.	Acting Sub-Lieutenant	**CH**	Heavy Cruiser
Asdic	Sonar acronym: Allied Submarine Detection and Investigation Committee	**CL**	Light Cruiser
		CD	Canada Decoration
		Cdr.	Commander
ASO	Anti-Submarine Officer	**CFB**	Canadian Forces Base
		CO	Commanding Officer
BB	Battleship	**Coxswain**	Senior Non-Commissioned Officer
Black Pit	Central Area of Atlantic Ocean not covered by air patrols		
		CPO	Chief Petty Officer
Bow	Front end of the ship	**CSL**	Canada Steamship Lines
Bravo Zulu	Naval expression of "well done"	**CV**	Aircraft Carrier
BTC	Convoy: Bristol Channel to the Thames River	**CVE**	Escort Aircraft Carrier
		CVL	Light Aircraft Carrier
Bulkhead	Walls or divisions between compartments in a ship		
		DC	Depth Charges
BX	Convoy: Boston to Halifax	**Deckhead**	Ceiling in a ship
		DD	Destroyer
CAF	Canadian Armed Forces	**DE**	Destroyer Escort

DND	Department of National Defence	**KMS**	Convoy: United Kingdom to the Mediterranean, *S* for slow
DSC	Distinguished Service Cross		
DW	Duty Watch		
		LCI	Landing Craft Infantry
EG	Escort Group	**LCM**	Landing Craft Medium
EO	Engineering Officer	**LCT**	Landing Craft Tank
ERA	Engine Room Artificer	**LS**	Leading Seaman
		LST	Landing Ship Tank
FAT	German pattern running torpedo	**Lt. or Lieut.**	Lieutenant, Air Force or Army
Fathom	Roughly 6 feet	**Lt.(N) or**	
FF	Frigate	**Lieut.(N)**	Lieutenant, Navy
FO	Flag Officer	**LCdr. or**	
Fo'c'sle	Forecastle, forward deck on a ship	**Lt. Cdr.**	Lieutenant Commander
Forward	Towards the front of a ship		
		MAC	Merchant Aircraft Carriers, designed to carry aircraft for convoy protection
Galley	Kitchen		
GO	Gunnery Officer		
Guns	Slang for Gunnery Officer	**MBE**	Member, Order of the British Empire
HE	High Explosive		
HF/DF	High Frequency Direction Finder	**Mess or**	
HH	Hedge Hog	**Messdecks**	Living space for the crew
HMS	His/Her Majesty's Ship	**Metox**	Early German radar
HMCS	His/Her Majesty's Canadian Ship	**MIA**	Missing in Action
HMTS	His/Her Majesty's Telegraph Ship	**MID**	Mentioned in Dispatches
Huff Duff	Slang for HF/DF	**Midship**	Toward the centre of a ship
HX	Convoy: Halifax or New York City to United Kingdom	**MKS**	Convoy: Mediterranean to United Kingdom, *S* for slow
		ML	Motor Launch
		MO	Medical Officer
I.O.D.E.	International Order of the Daughters of the Empire	**MOMP**	Mid-Ocean Meeting Point
		MTB	Motor Torpedo Boat
		MV	Motor Vessel
Jimmy	Slang for Executive Officer		
		NATO	North Atlantic Treaty Organization
KIA	Killed in Action	**NEF**	Newfoundland Escort Force
Killick	Slang for Leading Seaman	**NLCC**	Navy League Cadet Corps

NO	Navigating Officer
NOIC	Naval Officer in Charge
NORAD	North American Air Defence
NRE	Naval Research Establishment
NSHQ	Naval Service Headquarters
Old Man	Slang for captain of a ship
OS	Ordinary Seaman
ON	Convoy: United Kingdom to North America
ONS	Convoy: United Kingdom to North America, S for slow
OD or OOD	Officer-of-the-Day
OOW	Officer-of-the-Watch
PLUTO	Pipeline Under the Ocean
PO	Petty Officer
Port	Left
POW	Prisoner of War
RAS	Replenishment at Sea
RCAF	Royal Canadian Air Force
RCMP	Royal Canadian Mounted Police
RCSCC	Royal Canadian Sea Cadet Corps
RDF	Radio Direction Finder
RN	Royal Navy
RCN	Royal Canadian Navy
RCNR	Royal Canadian Navy Reserve
RCNVR	Royal Canadian Navy Volunteer Reserve
ROP	Report of Proceedings
R/T	Radio Transmitter, Voice
SBA	Sick Bay Attendant
SC	Convoy: Sidney NS to United Kingdom

SEF	Sidney Escort Force
Skipper	Slang for captain of a ship
SO	Senior Officer
SNO	Senior Naval Officer
SOE	Senior Officer of the Escort
SLt.	Sub-Lieutenant
SS	Steam Ship, but also Submarine
Starboard	Right
Stern	Back end of the ship
Tiffy	Slang for a sick bay attendant
U-boat	German Submarine
USN	United States Navy
USS	United States Ship
VE Day	Victory in Europe Day
VJ Day	Victory in Japan Day
Wardroom	Officers' mess in a ship
Wavy Navy	Slang for RCNVR
WA	Western Approaches
WAC	Western Approaches Command
WEF	Western Escort Force
Whaler	Ship's boat
WLEF	Western Local Escort Force
W/T	Wireless Transmitter, Radio Morse Code
WU	Working Up
XO	Executive Officer/Second in Command

BIBLIOGRAPHY

ARCHIVES

Library and Archives Canada: Records of the Department of National Defence, RG 24

    Volume 6889, File NSS 8870-332/109

        Sinking of HMCS *Trentonian*

    Volume 6911, File NSS 8970-332/109

        Working Up Programme, HMCS *Trentonian*

    Volume 4107, File 1156-332/109

        Report Board of Inquiry, Sinking of HMCS *Trentonian*

    Volume 11739, File CS 161-86-1

        Engagement of HMTS *Monarch* by USS *Plunkett*

        Monthly Report of Proceedings, May 1944

        Monthly Report of Proceedings, June 1944

        Naval Message from FOIC *Falmouth*

        Monthly Report of Proceedings, September 1944

        Report of Proceedings, Escort of Phoenix Convoy

    Volume 11755, File *Trentonian*, HMCS

        List of Survivors, HMCS *Trentonian*

    Volume 6761, File NSS 8180-331/67, HMCS *Napanee*, Collisions and Groundings

        Letter, L.W. Murray, Rear Admiral, Commander-in-Chief, Canadian Northwest Atlantic

    Volume 11563, File D.15-2-3, HMCS *Napanee*, Collisions and Groundings

        Letter, W.L. Puxley, A/Capt. (RN), Captain (D), Halifax

    Volume 6809, File NSC 8700-332/12, HMCS *Belleville*

        Movements

    Volume 11111, File 55-2-1/483, HMCS *Hallowell*

        HMCS *Somer Isle*

        Memorandum

    Volume 6763, File NSC 8180-381/16, HMCS *Hallowell*

        Memorandum to Hydrographer

    Volume 11561, File 8-23-3, HMCS *Hallowell*

        Naval Message

Volume 11108, File 55-2-1/175
   Grounding of HMCS *Quinte*

Volume 6766, File NS18180-443/51, Collisions and Groundings, HMCS *Quinte*
   Report Commanding Officer

   Survey HMCS *Quinte*

NAVY 4193, File 9430-MSC 149
   Fire Report, 16 October 1954, HMCS *Quinte*

   Fire Report, 3 March 1957, HMCS *Quinte*, 149

   Fire Report, 25 November 1960, HMCS *Quinte*, 149

Volume 4101, File 1151 FSE 169, Boards of Enquiry and Investigations

Collisions, Groundings and Damage, Collision of HMCS *Portage* with HMCS *Quinte*, Statement of LCDR D.P. Brownlow
   Collision of HMCS *Portage* with HMCS *Quinte*

   Report of the Board of Inquiry

Department of National Defence, Directorate of History and Heritage
   HMCS *Napanee*, File 81/520/8000, Box 67, File 7
      Ship's Movements

      History of HMCS *Napanee*

   HMCS *Belleville*, File 81/520/8000, Box 81, File 2
      Press Release, 11 June 1945

      Ship's Movements

      Report of Proceedings, 18 January to 20 January

   HMCS *Hallowell*, File 81/520/8000, Box 45, File 2
      A History of the Frigates HMCS *Strathadam*, *Hallowell*, *Violetta*

      Report of Proceedings of Escort Group C.1

      Herald, 29 March 1944

      Halifax Mail Star, "Naval Hero's Birthplace — An Unsettled Argument," 19 February 1960

HMCS *Quinte*, File 81/520/8000, Box 85, File 6

    Ship Movements

    A Brief History of HMCS *Quinte*, First of Name

    Message

    Report of Proceedings, Letter to Director of Operations Division

    Letter, Foundation Maritime Limited

    Groundings and Collisions

    Naval Message 12/02/45

HMCS *Quinte* (II), File 81/520/8000, Box 85, File 7

    Brief Narrative of HMCS *Quinte*, Second of Name

    Press Release, Launching Arrangements, AMC 149

    Announcement by Naval Headquarters, 17 May 1957

    Press Release, Shipyards Given Big Job, 25 April 1962

    Information from Crown Assets, 15 December 1971

HMCS *Quinte* (II), File 81/520/8000, Box 85, File 8

    Monthly Report, June 1956

    Monthly Report, June 1957

    Halifax *Chronicle Herald*, 31 March 1958

    Monthly Report of Proceedings, 31 March 1958

    Rescue Brings Commendation, Crowsnest, July 1959

    Commanding Officers Report, 8 December 1960

    Reports of Proceedings, Atlantic Command, November 1962

    Report of Proceedings, HMCS *Quinte*, January 1964

HMCS *Trentonian*, File 81/520/8000, Box 105, File 5

    Naval Message, 22 February 1945

    Jack Macbeth, "American Destroyer's Gunfire Smashed Cableship Namesake,"

    Ottawa *Journal*, 19 December 1953

    Loss of *Trentonian*, Press Release, 26 March 1945

Archives and Collections Society, Picton

Picton Gazette

"I.O.D.E. to Buy Ship's Bell for Frigate Hallowell," 12 April 1944

"Prince Edward County People …," 3 May 1944

"Sir Benjamin Hallowell Fought Under Nelson," 19 July 1944

"Organize Committee to Furnish Comforts for HMCS Hallowell," 19 July 1944

City of Quinte West Public Library

HMCS *Trentonian*, Hazel Farley Collection

Letter from W.E. Harrison, 17 December 1943

Excerpt of letter from W.E. Harrison, 25 May 1944

Letter from W.E. Harrison, 11 November 1944

Letter from W.E. Harrison, 11 July 1944

Letter from W.E. Harrison, 6 January 1945

Letter from W.E. Harrison, 25 January 1945

Mayor Sends Cable to Commander on Citizens Behalf

Article, "The Men Were Marvelous"

Magazines from Trenton on "Joliette"

Trenton Advocate

The Trentonian

"Skipper Recalls Trentonian Sinking," 7 May 1979

City of Belleville Public Library

Ontario *Intelligencer* Archive, "Impressive Ceremony Marks Acceptance of Comforts Supplied by Our Citizens," 23 October 1944

County of Lennox and Addington Museum and Archives

M. Fochuk, Stephen. *Remembering — Lennox & Addington Veterans of World War II and the Korean Conflict.* Lennox and Addington Historical Society: 2001

File HMCS *Napanee*

Marine Museum of the Great Lakes, Kingston, Ontario

Ken Macpherson, "Naval Shipbuilding on the Great Lakes, 1940–45," *FreshWater — A Journal of Great Lakes Marine History*, Vol. 3, No. 1, 1988

Maurice D. Smith, "Kingston Shipyards — World War II," *FreshWater — A Journal of Great Lakes Marine History*, Vol. 5 No. 1, 1990

Thunder Bay Public Library Archives,

The Fort William *Daily Times-Journal*

"Minesweeper *Quinte* Launched," 10 August 1953

"Shipyard to Build Second Naval Ship," 10 August 1953

"Warship Ceremony Is Held," 15 October 1954

"Minesweeper Squadron Seen in Manoeuvres," 12 June 1961

Maritime Command Museum, Halifax

File HMCS *Napanee*

File HMCS *Quinte* (II)

BOOKS

Benedet, David A. *Port Arthur Built: An Illustrated History of Port Arthur Shipbuilding Company*. Thunder Bay: Lehto Printers, n.d.

Bercuson, David J., and Holger H. Herwig. *Deadly Seas*. Toronto: Vintage Canada, 1998.

Douglas, W. A. B., Roger Sarty, and Michael Whitby. *No Higher Purpose*. St. Catharines, ON: Vanwell, 2002.

Freeman, David J. *Canadian Warship Names*. St. Catharines, ON: Vanwell, 2000.

German, Commander Tony. *The Sea Is at Our Gates*. Toronto: McClelland & Stewart, 1990.

Gregory, Walter. *Memories of HMCS* Trentonian *Alias K368: Trenton's Own Ship*. Trenton: Royal Canadian Legion, 1979.

Hague, Arnold. *The Allied Convoy System 1939–1945*. St. Catharines, ON: Vanwell, 2000.

Hopkins, Anthony. *Songs from the Front & Rear*. Edmonton: Hurtig Publishers, 1979.

Johnston, Mac. *Corvettes Canada*. Whitby, ON: McGraw-Hill Ryerson, 1994.

Lamb, James B. *On the Triangle Run*. Toronto: Macmillan of Canada, 1986.

Macbeth, Jack. *Ready Aye Ready*. Toronto: Key Porter, 1989.

Macpherson, Ken, and Marc Milner. *Corvettes of the Royal Canadian Navy 1939–1945* St. Catharines, ON: Vanwell, 1993.

Macpherson, Ken, and John Burgess. *The Ships of Canada's Naval Forces 1910–1913*. St. Catharines, ON: Vanwell, 1994.

Melady, John. *Explosion Trenton Disaster*. Belleville, ON: Mika, 1980.

Milner, Marc. *North Atlantic Run*. Toronto: University of Toronto Press, 1985.

_____. *The U-Boat Hunters*. Toronto: University of Toronto Press, 1994.

Paquette, E.R., and C.G. Bainbridge. *Honours & Awards, Canadian Naval Forces World War II*. Victoria: E.W. Bickle, 1986.

Schull, Joseph. *Far Distant Ships*. Toronto: Stoddart, 1950.

OTHER SOURCES

Private Collections

    Roger Glassco, Son of Lieutenant Commander Colin Glassco, RCNVR

    Robert F.D. Hall, Son of Mayor Hall and Mrs. Duane Hall of Napanee

    Sam Andrews, Grandson of Eric Troops, RNR (ret), HMTS *Monarch*

    Walter Gregory, Author, Member of Branch 110, Trenton Royal Canadian Legion

USS *Plunkett* Association

    Ship's Log, USS *Plunkett*

Royal Canadian Sea Cadet Corps Quinte, Belleville

    HMCS *Belleville*, Ship's History

    HMCS *Quinte*, Ship's History

    HMCS *Quinte* (II), Ship's History

Navy League Cadet Corps Trentonian, Trenton

    File HMCS *Trentonian*, Honour Roll

    File HMCS *Trentonian*, Ship's History

OF RELATED INTEREST

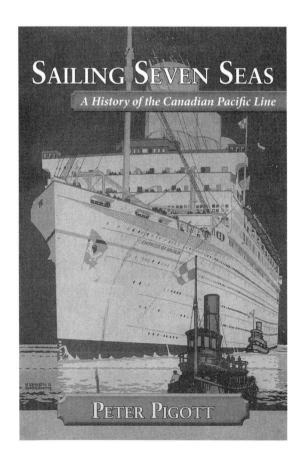

Sailing Seven Seas
by Peter Pigott
978-1554887651
$35 £23

Under Canadian Pacific's red-and-white-checkered flag, the company's founders, George Stephen and William C. Van Horne, created a rail/sea service from Liverpool to Hong Kong. Boasting sternwheelers, Great Lakes bulk carriers, ferries, and luxurious ocean-going liner leviathans, the Canadian Pacific shipping line sailed around the globe. In both world wars the entire fleet served gallantly as Allied troop carriers. After the Second World War, the company staved off the realities of the jet age for as long as it could, replacing liners with container ships, until what was left of the legendary maritime operation was sold off in 2005.

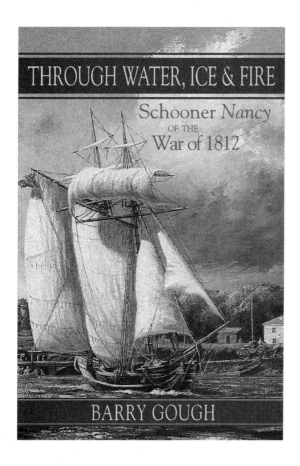

Through Water, Ice & Fire
by Barry Gough
978-1550025699
$24.99 £12.99

The schooner *Nancy*, legendary vessel of Great Lakes and Canadian history, lived a thousand lives in a noted career that began in Detroit and ended in a fiery explosion in Nottawasaga River in the last year of the War of 1812.

This dramatic, soundly researched narrative depicts the reality of the men who sailed her while fighting a gritty war. Carrying the war to the enemy in hazardous ways, they fought against a powerful American foe, using stealth and daring to maintain the besieged Canadian position in the last armed struggle for the heartland of North America. The loss of the *Nancy* inspired generations to regard her as a symbol of devotion to king and country.